Chronicles
of the
New Jack Era

To My Brother
Perry from Gerald
G Money

Resurrection

of G' Money

The Chronicles of The New Jack Era books may be ordered through booksellers or by contacting us at gmentertainment1book@gmail.com.

Copyright © 2014 gmentertainment1
Cover design-Hotbookcovers.com
Book editing-Tina M. Alfano
Front and back cover pictures-Dan Myricks
ISBN: 978-0-615-94161-5
Printed in the United States of America

Dedication

I'd like to dedicate this book to my mom who gave me life. To God who should be given all the glory. `

To all of my family and friends with sincere appreciation for always being in my corner and always believing in me.

Special Thanks

Tina M. Alfano
Jordan T. Alfano
Belinda Weber
Tyesha Riddick
Creflo Dollar (My mentor)
David Parks
Michael Walker
DJ Smitty Rock
Ruff Ryders
Ralph Matthews
Sal Freud
Stephanie Brady
Dora Brown
Jamal Thomas
Big King Boss
Monique Danielle
Tina White
Rodney Stone
Reggie Johnson and Beryl Brown
Sabrina Jackson

Table of Contents

CHRONICLES OF THE NEW JACK ERA

Introduction

In the beginning, I didn't realize the effect my life would have on society. After many years of silence, I now feel the time has come to tell the world the truth about my story so others can learn from it. Understand that Hollywood with its magician like touch can take the most ruthless gangster one could imagine and turn that person into a character people would love, mimic and idolize. How many people do we know with a poster up in their home from The Godfather™, The Mack™, Scarface™, New Jack City™, The Devil's Double™, etc? That is the magic of Hollywood but reality is sometimes the exact opposite. Think about how many people have been killed and lives destroyed from trying to walk in the footsteps of these Pimps, Dons and Gangsters. That's because when you don't have all the facts and rules in this game of life and money, it's easy to slip and fall. Mistakes are bound to take place when there is no direction. Unemployment is high and so many are scraping at the bottom that want to be successful and on top. Can you feel why the time is right for me to shed some light on the booby traps so more of my brothers and sisters can rise up to the divinity GOD intended for them. "Am I not my brother's keeper?"! That's why it's time to expose the New Jack Era.

Allow me to introduce myself. My name is G'Money: Good Money, Gave Money, Got Money and going to get a lil' more money! Ha Ha, I'm only serious! That's right. You are reading the true story of G'Money from New Jack City™. Check this: New Jack City™, supposedly fictitious tale, was actually based on real life events, places and individuals who were reared in Harlem located at the top of Money Making Manhattan. I was running the streets during the time of Studio 54, Crack and the birth of Hip Hop. Although there was no Carter Hotel there was a group called CMB aka Cash Money Brothers, and there was a "Nino Brown" and also "G'Money" (funny thing is I look a lot more like Wesley Snipes then Nino did) and we did run and use all kinds of drugs. You might wonder how a guy like me survived that kind of life? Don't worry; we will cover in detail how, when and why later in the book. I'm not proud of everything I did. Fortunately, it seems the set back was for the comeback.

My tale is not an easy one to tell. It's filled with a lot of heartache, blood, pain, sweat, tears and suffering that I caused not only to others but to myself as well. In reading this, I give you a testimony on how you can gain the wealth and power to sit up, stand up and fly after you get down. SAY IT LOUD! Can I get an Amen! G'money is here to show the strength of the human spirit and how God's plan moves us through the good, the bad and the ugly. Had it not been for God's mercy I would not he here today to share my secrets. I'm only serious! Serious like a heart attack!

I recognize that I'm here and I exist today because God allowed me to be here. And through my testimony I will show you how you can learn to change your current life the way it is today and walk in the way of righteousness instead of walking in the way of the world.

That brings me to lesson number one: A wise man walks with GOD. In my youth, I didn't really get that. Riches would come and go. Then I'd find myself hustling again to chase after that golden calf. Each time I'd get a little more but soon after I would lose more than I had the time before. Eventually this cycle ended with me homeless and in jail like a baby thrown in the crib for acting up. It wasn't until I put away my childish thoughts and ways that this important lesson really sunk into me and took hold. I'm not saying you have to stop having fun to gain and maintain power, wealth, love and stability. All I'm saying is if you want the party to keep going without it getting shot up or shut down, GOD better be on your guest list. Living just enough for the city isn't cutting it anymore. You hear what I'm telling you? I'm only serious! Ha Ha!

Now that I have been resurrected back on top, it is through the act of redemption that I write The Chronicles of the New Jack Era. This book is for all mankind to view and understand what I went through. I had been born into such a privileged life. Had anyone told me that I would travel some of the roads that would lead me to a life of crime, drugs and deception only to be born again into a life filled with the love of GOD, I would have thought them crazy. Now as a man having lived through being taken advantage of by temptation, I am reborn with a sense of compassion and responsibility for myself and others. Understand that as the human race evolves, everyone must repent by acknowledging the roles they play that affected their environment. You must have the courage to look at reality for what it is. When we allow truth to renew our mind, we gain a change of heart. Your new heart will attract what you need to live the abundant life that is filled with wealth, love and purpose.

There is an abundant way of living out there awaiting you and I but you have to find the keys; and prepare your way for greatness as I am today. All it takes is for you to allow God to put his super on your natural and you will be restored.

The first thing that you have to do is change your mind set. Once you understand the importance of changing your frame of mind, you will learn the keys to redemption.

Changing your frame of mind is important, especially in the day and times that we live in today. There is always so many things happening in society, and sometimes people just want to be accepted, and entertain the wrong type of company and get caught up in things of the world. But God wants to remind us of our purpose. No man is perfect and every man has sinned and done things because of the temptations of the world. But there is a way out. You can repent and you can be forgiven, you can renew your frame of mind and you can be redeemed.

Redemption is free for you and me. You may have made many mistakes and may have done some things in your life that you are not proud of. You might have had people that talked about you and ridiculed you and you may feel ashamed, but everything will be alright if you let God into your heart; God loves us all and he is willing to forgive us and give us another chance. I have learned these lessons through the experience of my redemption. Once I surrendered I felt free. I was able to love the unlovely and able to forgive people and see past whatever transpired. I learned how to walk in the love of God. And love endures all things. I have humbled my spirit and I now walk in the knowledge of the word. What does the word have to say about the matter? The world can give you whatever you desire...but who will save your soul?

Now I have put away the old man and do not represent who I use to be. I walk with the renewed mind in the belief of the manifestation of God. Nothing is by chance, everything happens for a reason. There is always a divine intervention accessible. Ask and you will receive peace within your soul that you have never experienced in your life.

With this new frame of mind how could I enjoy seeing the lives of others being driven and used like pawns on a chess board. There was no way that I could live that way anymore and I have come to realize that the purpose of man is to be born again. To discover the word of God. Once it is time to leave this world, you will have experienced failure through mistakes but altered HIS way of thinking by searching for knowledge and wisdom through the word of God. That once his purpose is fulfilled and he has completed the tests that life presents through trials and tribulations that he would be redeemed and become obedient to the B.I.B.L.E. (Which initials stand for "Biblical instructions before leaving Earth"). This book presents a chance for you the reader to learn the precious secrets I've acquired over the years. It will also help you avoid some of the mistakes I made along the way to the top. From lil' G to Ol' G, the truth shall be told as you read. Grow a little wiser on this crazy ride that will leave you entertained and amazed. That's me- G'Money. "Good Money, Gave Money, Got Money and going to get a lil' more money while teaching you how to get some too. Read on...

And by the way, names have been changed to protect the innocent inside this book!

Chapter 1
Little G

Before I became the infamous G'Money known in the streets of Harlem to the streets of Hollywood and around the world, I was a straggly little kid growing up in a time that offered more opportunities in life then most kids had in Harlem at the time. The Harlem I know and love is a place where the legitimate Black movers and shakers of Black culture in New York City lived. It was where the NAACP was located, fractions of the Black Panther Party, Children from the Marcus Garvey movement, Cotton Club and the National Black Theatre. It was a haven for the BBC- Black Beautiful Celebrities. People like Rap Brown lived right in the same building with Honey Cole and Atkinson who hosted the famous Apollo Theatre when I was growing up. The Radio personality from 107.5 WBLS, "Eddie O'Jay" also lived in Harlem. The singing group called The Black Ivory, Barbara Anne Teer and the owner of the National Black Theatre all lived there too. Walking the streets you would run into some of the original B-Boy Dancers like Pee Wee Dance and Rerun from that show "What's Happening™". Harlem was the place to be if you were Black. It was as if the Harlem Renaissance never died from my point of view. There were so many good opportunities for Black people at that time. It made me very proud to walk down the street and be able to collaborate with some of the most influential Black celebrities I knew in show business!

Of course, the most infamous personality of all residing in Harlem was me, Lil' G.! I grew up in Esplanade Gardens, a co-op apartment complex that expanded from 145th Street and Lenox Avenue (also known as Malcolm X Boulevard) to 148th Street and 7th Avenue. This complex was and still is the embalmment of the Black Harlem Community. A community secured with guards, private parking for its residents, swimming pools, private playgrounds and all other sorts of amenities that made life easier and more secure for the people who resided there. It was so safe that my strict mother felt it was ok for me to run around with my little friends in the building without supervision.

Let me tell you something about my momma. First thing, she was gorgeous! Her hair was always done... My momma was the sweetest but if you got caught doing wrong you could kiss your behind goodbye! If she had any idea what I was getting into when I left the house she would have locked me up in my room and thrown away the key until I was 30 something! Don't get me started on what my Father would have done. Remember I grew up in a time when getting a whooping was still politically correct. My point is that in such a privileged environment why would they suspect a thing? How could they know my path would cause me to choose the bright lights of street night life, the darkness and perils in the ghettos of Harlem and the riches of Satan's material world? Man if they had any idea what I was up to, I would have been shipped in reverse back to Cuba! Y ju don't know?! I'm only serious, Ha Ha!

Yeah thinking back, my spoiled little behind didn't realize or appreciate how good I had it. You know my mother always wanted the best for me. She seriously spoiled me rotten. I mean at 8 years old my allowance was so much a week; I don't want to tell you the amount, it would only make you mad your parents never gave you that much money when you were my age. She dressed me in the best shoes and clothes money could buy. Any toy I wanted I got. My mother wanted to duplicate what she didn't have and apply that to my life so that I could learn how to have it. I must say my mother was right about how you teach your child to obtain the material things that make life comfortable. She seriously spoiled me.

The only hitch was that she did it without any spiritual base. My Mother never told me about GOD. Her Momma was a Christian though, a believer of GOD. Hopefully your Momma's Momma taught her about GOD and then, as my Grandmother used to say, "Baby bring that child up in a way that he will never depart from GOD." That's probably why my Momma was such a nice person, but since she didn't preach that stuff to me I started out on the wrong foot. The seed she planted was a blessing and a curse. My Mother never knew that I would become a man that others would emulate and make movies about. Neither did I! I mean, this is the child my Momma had. All I know is that she instilled a drive in me to maintain the lifestyle that she provided. I grew up expecting and wanting it all. I wanted it and I got it at any expense.

It took many years of experience to learn that GOD has a major role in this whole thing. Listen carefully, prayer without action is a waste of time. How many people do we know sitting at home praying for money and stay broke because they won't get off their butts and do some work. I mean at least go buy a lottery ticket and win 2 dollars! Ha Ha, I'm only serious... The important point here is that action without prayer is worse. Action without prayer is what leaves you open to the pitfalls in life like work. You don't enjoy it so it drains you. Drugs that can kill you, depression, thievery, murder and sexual exploitation can make you feel the same way. No one is saying you shouldn't have fun or nice things. You should aim to be a King Solomon, Bill Gates or Michael Jackson. Till this day I can't sleep just anywhere or wear just anything. I like looking good, living well and respecting myself like the divine child of GOD we all are. Just don't lose sight of what's important. You have to know GOD for yourself to figure out what that is to you.

As kids we don't know jack. We are just getting to know ourselves while taking in our environments like super sponges. So on one side I had my Mother teaching me to love the taste of richness and on the other side I had my Father. Now you think I was spoiled? You should have seen the way my Momma took care of that man. My Moms followed and obeyed my Father. She knew what a black man had to go through in the world and she was going to be his guardian angel. She was like Coretta Scott King working with her husband, a man of power that was developing and aiming to become commissioner of New York City. You know how they say, "behind every great man there is a greater woman"? My Moms was that woman. She made sure my Dad didn't have any problems. Whatever he wanted, she made sure that he was comfortable. She never did anything that would jeopardize his position and she did her best to make sure no one else did either. She did this because he was motivated and ambitious. He took care of business at home, was a good provider and he was blessed with good looks.

We didn't do things together as a family. This wasn't the Beaver Clever house. My parents did not bring me up that way. We didn't have game night in my house. We didn't even go to church together but man my Dad was cool! Can you imagine a black man in the early 70's being the Deputy Chief Officer of a Fire Department in New York City? He was living large and in charge. White men had to obey his orders. They couldn't even take a piss without asking his permission! The thing I liked most was how power didn't seem to corrupt him at all. He was good to his wife and he was always cool, calm and collected. There was hardly ever a moment when I didn't see him trying to better himself. He got to that position at work by studying and working hard. He paid no attention to what the world told black men they could not be at the time. I watched him work his way up from Captain to Lieutenant to Battalion and then

Deputy Chief. The next step after that was Commissioner and he was shooting at that target.

When he studied, we all had to be extremely quiet. As with a lot of kids, when I was young, being quiet was a bit of a challenge for me. Instead of getting upset, my Dad would say, "Pick up a book and read it!"

I thank him for this every day because some of the best tricks and rules of the trade in this life I learned out of books. In any business, whether you work for yourself or someone else, there are four main ingredients needed to cook up success. First and foremost, as my Dad showed me, your education should never stop. A wise man is always learning. Living with my Dad and seeing him in action taught me the other three: you must have confidence aka self-esteem, you must have a good work ethic and you must have perseverance. Because of my Dad's efforts, his pockets were always fat. My mother had her way of spoiling me and my Dad's way was showing me that in his house money was not an object. Man I had the kind of allowance you could buy guns with.

All my little friends in Esplanade Gardens got money from their parents like I did. Including a kid named Barry Cooper that grew up to be co-writer on the classic movie "New Jack City™". Growing up with money does something to you. You're not afraid to aim for greatness because that is the norm for you. Look at Donald Trump who owns half the casino world if not more. Or look at Barak Obama who became America's first Black president who grew up on an island where it's so beautiful you can't help feeling rich. In some ways it can be worse than coming from the ground up because when things hit the fan you don't know how to survive without. There was a great prince that killed himself because when things went down in the Middle East, his family lost money and he had to come to New York to get a job. Can you believe that? Killing yourself because your parents told you that you have to get a job? Some of you might think that's crazy talk but I understand how that can happen. I had no concept of poverty or how low you could fall until it happened to me. If I wasn't willing to learn and if my grandmother didn't plant that seed of GOD in me so I would be receptive to it when it came, I might be dead now too.

Sometimes when you have so much, it makes you crazy, cruel and insensitive to those without and you don't even know it. I still remember how different things were when my Mother would take me over to my cousin's house that lived in the projects. They ate the peanut butter from welfare that was in a can. It wasn't like Jiffy and Skippy, they had to stir their welfare peanut butter up. Of course my smart mouth had to point that out to them. I was also fascinated how their welfare cheese came in long brown box and you had to cut it with a knife. I'm sure they thought I was mocking them but the truth is I didn't know any better. I also remember being over at their house for breakfast. They used to take the oatmeal in a bowl and they didn't even cook it. They just stir it up and put sugar on it and sing as they fed it to me, "Life could never be exactly like you want it to be but you'll be satisfied".

As a kid I just thought, "This is good! Mmmmmmmmm, it's sweet!" I didn't realize they were mocking me, but I deserved it. When my cousins would come to my house I had to show off. I had everything. I had my own bathroom. I had my own bedroom, my own wall unit with a music entertainment system, including, my own closet. I had two beds in case my cousins wanted to sleep over and I had my own television set. I was doing my thing. To make matters worse, when they would come over to my house a week or two days before Easter, I really acted up. It was this time of year that my Mother would give my cousins the old clothes she bought me since I had new ones from the holidays. I would protest, "Momma not the grey suit! I like that suit, Momma! Why their momma can't buy them a suit? Why they always take my stuff?" I didn't realize until I got older how that dynamic must have affected them.

The projects, the streets, the guns, the drugs... in my real life fantasy world it was all a game to me. I was so separated from it that I was fearless which eventually turned into me being mischievous. That coupled with my gift for gab turned me into the Devil's son. I was an average student in school but I was also an incredibly good communicator. Yours truly, Lil' G, was able to hide behind my mouth for a long time. Parents just didn't see me being a troublemaker. I was the kind of kid who could go to his friend's house right after they were put on punishment and still get to see them. I would show up at their house and be like, "Mrs. So-and-so can Billy come out and play?"

The mother would suck her teeth at me, "Boy, you know Billy is on punishment!"

I would just stand there in one of the sharp looking outfits my Mother bought me and smile at my friend's mom with my cute little dark chocolate drop face and big brown puppy dog eyes.

Then Mrs. So and So would think for a second, smile and say, "Gerald get in here because I know you're not going anywhere until you see Billy."

This was an example of utilizing the art of persistence which I learned earlier and remember; persistence goes a long way.

Amongst my peers, things were very different. In school I always found myself in minor altercations because even though it was a private school, it was still a place where kids from many walks of Harlem life came together. Some kids called me square because of the way I dressed. Others called my black ass white because of the way I spoke or rich because of where I lived. They didn't know who they were messing with. I wasn't gonna be punked by anybody. Understand something, G'Money today just like Lil' G back in the day wasn't having it. My Father and Uncle taught me young that if I didn't want to get picked on for most of my life, I better defend myself when attacked.

Now me, Lil' G, took that lesson to a whole 'nother level. Let me give you an example. One day when I was at school, the teacher left the class room and I started performing and mimicking her and my classmates started laughing hysterically, they were laughing so much until tears started coming out their eyes and they couldn't stop laughing. By the time the teacher got back, everything was back to normal and none was the wiser... that is until two punk boys went to tattle tale on me with their big mouths The teacher was humiliated because when she came back in the class room, she had a look on her face like she suspected something had gone down and she was trying to figure out what had took place when she left the class. After discovering I was impersonating her; the teacher got so upset over what I did that she went to the principal and I got suspended. That move on their part sowed the seed of revenge in me so deep it was war! I mean not only was I suspended because they ratted on me after they started it, I felt really bad seeing the looks on my parents faces after they worked so hard to get me into that school. Let's not even talk about the punishment that followed. There was no way Lil' G was gonna let it end like that!

I had plenty of time to plan during the suspension just how I would get them back for what they did. Eventually I got my opportunity and took it. After several days being kept inside, my Momma finally let me go out because she needed me to go to the store for her.

"Come right back!" She said

I said, "O.k. Momma." with a smile but instead of going directly to the store, I ran every bit of 22 blocks to the school I got suspended from. School had just let out. I proceeded to inquire about the whereabouts of the boys I was looking for. Someone told me they were already on a bus that was 4 blocks away. I began to chase that bus. Thank GOD city buses are so damn slow and have lots of stops. I caught up with the bus, boarded it and spotted the two punks I was looking for. You should have seen their faces! I ran over to them and commenced in kicking their you know what! Once the whooping was complete, I quickly got off of the bus, ran back towards my house, stopped at the store for my mother's groceries, then I went home and made sure to catch my breath before walking in. Needless to say the boys reported the beating to the school officials. I didn't care, I was already suspended. The icing on the cake was how my Mother vehemently stood by my side with me, professing my innocence explaining to the officials that it couldn't have possibly been me because I was at the store and she had the groceries to prove it. She also went on to tell them they should look into what those boys are doing since so many people feel the need to beat them up. Yes, that was one of my sweet victories.

Time off from school probably wasn't the best thing for me because it allowed me to get closer to my other spoiled rich, up to no good friends in my building. There was Russell, Stacey, Cedric, Dewayne and Red. People grew to know us as the E.G. Boys because we all lived in Esplanade Gardens. We were tight and always looking for fun and trouble.

Well, Russell, we called him Liar for short because he was a habitual liar! He always got us mixed up in some crazy mess. Stacey aka Pretty Boy Smooth, was the prettiest looking kid alive. The girls loved him. He looked like...well...let's just say Michael Jackson couldn't touch him. He had a way about him that made you want to be around him.

Cedric was my ace boon coon. He had a lot of mouth but could back it up. Ced could have been a star athlete if he wanted, or the president of Harlem. He always had this swagger of a conqueror.

Then there was Red. Now Red was my best friend but he was also the slowest brother in the world! If Red was riding shotgun he'd still get there late. One time he had me waiting.... just because...

I spent most of my free time with the E.G. Boys. Sometimes Red would bring his little brother Piper. Piper was cool. Anyway we used to run the streets like we owned them. There were only six of us (sometimes eight) but after we put our skills, swag and allowances together, we were the baddest bunch on the block. We'd do stuff like sneak into the Apollo Theatre, go shopping, bowling... Everyone noticed us especially the pimps and pushers. They couldn't figure out how some young cats like us were rolling as good as we all were!!

The E.G. Boys were closer then blood and bad as a bat out of hell. The thing is, we were following the idol figures of the world. We wanted to be and live like The Godfather™, Scarface™, Super Fly™ and The Mack™. We didn't have to beg, steal or borrow anything because our parents provided us with everything but we still yearned for the street life. The 70's were all about sex, drugs and disco.

To tell you the truth it wasn't just the movies that influenced us. We learned all the things in the world like sex, drinking and smoking from watching our family and relatives. You know the Bible warns us about certain individuals, including those in your family. I know I had an Aunt that had nobody teaching her what she needed to know in order to teach her children where they could grow up knowing about redemption and the other things of GOD. Instead, when I checked her out I noticed a slugger who had no chief, no ruler and no overseer.

She was on her own and would say things like, "I don't want nobody to tell me what to do. What? Tell ME!? This is my house!"

To a kid that's what freedom is all about man! Let's talk about sex too, baby. Do you think that I would have had sex so early knowing that I could have waited until marriage to have something special and magical with someone solely devoted to being with me? O.k. Jokers... yes there are those that would argue that point about me, but in reality I lost that game before it even started. My Uncle Little Jap who had a spot right down the block took care of that. They called my Uncle Little Jap because he had chinky eyes and was almost as small as I was at the time.

Little Jap was constantly saying things to me like, "Go on boy, you hit that?" while walking around with two to three girls at a time that were half his age and loved flirting with me.

My Uncle was a big influence in teaching the E.G. Boys the importance of having a trade. Little Jap was from the south and he was uneducated because he couldn't read or write. What stood out to us though was that even though he was uneducated, he still found a way to make lots of money. How did he do it? Little Jap had two jobs. One was as a Carpenter/ Brick Mason. We learned by watching him level cement with his hands. It wasn't the conventional way but he was good at what he did so it brought in money. His second job was running a "shooting gallery" in the spot he had down the block. Don't get it twisted; he didn't have us kids around a bunch of trigger happy nut cases. This wasn't your typical shooting gallery. I guess the type of shooting that was going on wasn't good for us to be around either. Fiends would give him a dollar to go down in his basement and shoot dope. He would chain up the fence leading downstairs to the shooting gallery whenever the cops came by. When they left he would open up the chain again. He would have about 15 to 20 junkies at a time giving him a dollar per hit. Now that's what you call a hustle. Eventually things started to go bad and he had to stop because some of the people would go down and never come back up. Aside from all that, if you think about it, my Uncle was a genius. That's why I always saw him with large stacks of singles. He might have been short with two slits for eyes but since he had money he had the girls and respect. Money definitely made a difference in his life and I was determined to have lots of it in mine.

There I was with the E.G. Boys deciding to be grown as a child. Yeah I was grown before I grew up. I knew what I wanted but I was still trying to figure out how I would get it on my own. That brings me to Ms. G. Ms. G was this nice neighbor that was friends with my Mother. Looking back at that time, I realize my personal success all started with her.

One day my Mother sent me out to the store for Ms. G. When I got back with the groceries, I decided to take a look at her library since my Dad was always telling me to read something. Ms. G was an educator and a very informative person. She really wanted the best for me. That day it was like she tapped right into my brain and could see what I needed. There she was standing next to me looking at the books. Ms. G asked me if there was anything I liked. Suddenly my eyes caught the title, "Think and Grow Rich™".

When I showed interest, she pulled it out and gave it to me saying, "Good choice."

I asked her what it was about. She advised me to take it home, read it and when I was done to come back so we could talk about it. I read that book and by the time I was done it had "transformed me". My life has never been the same since. By the time I got back to Ms. G, I was filled with questions and she was ready with the answers. Together she helped me analyze that book and put its knowledge to good use. It seems like since that day Ms. G gave me that book, Ms. G had impacted my life in everything that I have ever done. She planted the first seed in every endeavor I've ever been involved in. As a matter of fact Ms. G still advises me to this day and she never forgets to commend me on every successful endeavor I accomplish. I have grown to love that woman as if she was my own moms.

So now you know how I found my yellow brick road. That book, "Think and Grow Rich™" by Napoleon Hill was the first stone in my personal temple of success. It guided me to realize my first occupation. Everyone has something they were born with, a special gift GOD has given you for the sole purpose of being self-sustainable no matter what time, era or age you live in. Once you tap into that thing people will throw money at you. This is important because you need to understand your great strengths in order to make real money. My gift was comedy, but I took it to the next level because I also specialized in doing impersonations.

Chapter 2
Laugh 'til You Drop

Most people don't realize this about me but G'Money had money before making money on the streets. Yeah, I had my own before getting into the drug hustle business. I may have been a teenager but my stand-up career as a comedian was impressive. Top-notch clubs requested me, I was on television and I had many celebrities from the screen and streets as personal friends.

Now my parents used to always have company at the house. The type of men that they kept around inspired me to go into comedy. When guests came to the house, it was usually late at night and so my Mother would send me to bed before the party started... right? I would play along and after getting tucked in, as soon as she left the room I would sneak and listen to their conversations with my ear to the bedroom door. One of the guys that always came over was such a joker that every time he was in the house I got in trouble. I mean this man had me laughing until my stomach and jaw hurt. Really I couldn't stop laughing and unknowingly snitched on myself because I was supposed to be asleep.

My Momma would yell, "Boy, didn't I tell you to go to bed? I ain't playing in here now. Don't make me come in there with my belt!"

I would be like, "Momma, I can't help it! I can't stop laughing!"

This guy was so quick with his jokes. I couldn't stop laughing even if I wanted to. That dude was funnier than Red Foxx, Flip Wilson and Rudy Ray Moore. I mean this boy was no joke and he inspired me.

During the summer I got to experiment with this gift that was awakening in me. My Mother used to send me to camp for five weeks every year between July and August. At that time I didn't have my own style as a comedian so I would impersonate other people like that guy from my house and celebrities I liked. One of the people I started impersonating was James Brown. I became star struck the first time I saw James Brown perform at the Apollo Theatre when I was an adolescent and man that guy was Mr. Dynamite himself. James Brown's music was so exciting; it made your heart rate go faster just listening to it! Kind of reminded me of the little girls at summer camp with their hot pants on. As he shuffled, spun and glided across the stage, I watched in complete awe and amazement. I decided that night of his concert that I wanted to be just like him. If I ever got the chance to perform I was going to make the crowd go crazy just like he had done! At the end of his performance I got close enough to James Brown for him to shake my hand AND HE DID! OH MY GOD! Hallelujah! It was over then! Man that really blew my mind so much so that when I got home that night I didn't want to wash that hand ever!

After that day I learned every single one of James Brown's songs. "I Feel Good", "Get Up", "I'm Black and I'm Proud", "Sex Machine"... you name it I got it down! Then I practiced this move in my room with one of them real old-fashioned microphones. First I would take the microphone and throw it up in the air. Then just when it looked like it was about to fall, I would step on the wire and catch the mic in my hand! To me it looked and felt like something James Brown would do.

So here I was, Lil' G at the coed summer camp and I wanted to impress the girls. By now I had perfected my James Brown impression and was ready. All the kids were around me and I took my chance. I did that move and maaaaan I tore the camp out! The girls went crazy! After that night every girl in there wanted to hook up with me. I was the man of the hour, animal tamer head park ranger. Man I never knew performing would give me such a rush. When I got back home I was quick to show my new found talent to the E.G. Boys, my friends at school, the members of my family and their friends. I enjoyed the response so much I decided to go to the Frank Garcia School of Magic. Once I incorporated magic into my comedy, it was a wrap! I studied hard and made sure my show was off the chain.

The E.G. Boys, my peers from school and the streets were my greatest supporters and audience. I was entering contests and doing comedy for them in our neighborhood development during the regular school year when I wasn't away at camp. Kids would wait for me to get home just to hear me tell jokes or do tricks. I learned this trick where I would take a lit cigarette and make it disappear into a handkerchief. To amp it up I started doing it with people's coats and other clothing!

When the cigarette was gone and it didn't leave a hole they would say, "Gerald, where did the cigarette go?"

I'd say, "I didn't learn that part of the trick yet."

They'd go crazy yelling, "Do that again! Do that again!"

Then I'd reply, "A magician only does his tricks once. Don't you know that fool?"

People would fall out laughing. I knew I was good so I kept going with it. Competition got intense but I stuck it out. Can you believe I was a teenager competing against college students and other adults? I remember one night at the Minisink Park Stage PA Talent Show, the announcer kept trying to psych me out.

He kept saying things like, "You ready young blood?" and "That crowd is going to eat you alive."

The UCLA Boys went on before me and they were good. I almost cracked but my friends came through for me. Whenever I got nervous the E.G. Boys were right there to keep pushing me on.

Stacey would say something like, "Yo snap out of it man..."

Then Dewayne would bring me back to reality by saying, "Come on G! You're next! Yo G!"

This particular night I really needed them because as the UCLA Boys were walking off and I was going onto the stage, one of cupid's arrows flew right out of the audience and smacked me right in the face. There sitting smack dab in the middle of the stands was Michelle and her boyfriend. I didn't care what her man was doing at the time but Michelle stood out like a beacon in the night. She was one of those girls from the neighborhood that everyone wanted but no small fry like me could have. That's when my Uncle Little Jap popped into my head. If I could just impress her with this show and make that money, I might have a chance.

Red grabbed me and yelled, "Yo G, you're up next man! Go do your thing."

I was determined to blow their minds like I did with the kids at my first performance at the summer camp, so I rocked it! I pulled all the stops. There was the comedy, the magic and then I hit them with my Gomer Pyle, Richard Nixon, Red Foxx and Richard Pryor impressions. The crowd was rolling! Most importantly there was a permanent smile stuck to Michelle's face that her man didn't put there. I was on top of the world. For me there was only one way to go from here and that was up.

Now that show gave me the confidence I needed to try out for Amateur Night at the Apollo. You should have seen me back then. The suit I wore was given to me by one of the biggest numbers runners in Harlem. He knew I was good so he sponsored me. With the suit, I wore a huge Jackson 5 afro. Man I looked funny but I spun it in a way that I also looked really good for the ladies. At first I didn't tell anyone I was performing. Being the best was how I wanted my friends and family to think of me always. Keeping my debut at the Apollo on the low seemed like the best thing to do in case I got booed off by the Sandman or something. It was hard keeping it a secret but I found ways to study, practice and do shows on my spare time.

When they introduced me, I came out and I touched the famous tree stump for good luck. As I mentioned earlier, doing a show on the same stage James Brown graced with his presence was a dream of mine. It happened just like the book "Think and Grow Rich™" said it would. First came the desire, the want. Then the "want" motivated me to put in the work and study, all the while knowing one day I would get what I wanted. Finally here I was at the Apollo in front of hundreds of people with the opportunity to win and entertain the crowd. When the rules in that book first work for you the feeling is unbelievable. To think I made this happen for myself just by believing it could happen for me. I paused for a moment to imagine a picture of the audience really loving my show. My heart was pounding in my chest and I knew I was ready.

My opening act was an impression of Donald Duck. As soon as I started all the black folk took off and started laughing. That's when my confidence set in and I knew I had them so I said, "My next impression will be... Paul Lynn."

Now I don't know if you remember that Coca Cola ™ commercial from the late 70's. It was a song that went something like, "Look up America and see what I got. I got a million more to blow. More songs to sing; more of the real thing... Coke!"

Most of the people in the audience must have been sniffing cocaine back in the day because that was the funniest thing anyone could have come out singing. The way the crowd kept roaring for me felt so good I was inspired. Next thing I found myself saying, "All the way from Las Vegas Nevada...Here's the multi-talented, Mr. Dynamite himself... Ladies and Gentlemen-JAAAAAAAAAAAMES BROOOOWWWN!" The Apollo band hit it and awe man! I went into my James brown impersonation microphone trick and all. Yo I tore 'em up! I WON AMATEUR HOUR! I WON FIRST PRIZE!!

I went home feeling so proud with that envelope filled with money. All I could think to say when my mother opened the door was, "Look ma, I won first prize at the amateur night at the Apollo!"

Everyone was so happy for me. When I got around to telling the E.G. Boys the next day, they practically threw me a parade. Their first reactions gave me material to work with for weeks. Dewayne with his old man face practically pissed his pants. Russell and his lying behind tried to convince me he was there and was waving to me from the balcony. Cedric slapped me so hard on my back that my eyes nearly popped out of my head. Then Cedric picked me up on his shoulders while Stacey Pretty Boy Smooth started Hee Heeing and doing the moon walk! Ha ha…. I'm only serious… Laughing around with all my friends I realized Red was so slow in his response but I could tell that he was the happiest for me just by the look on his face. His delayed reaction was a simple thumbs up and a wink.

Let me tell you I was on a roll. I went back to the Apollo and won first prize again and again! Me and the E.G. Boys lived like kings for the next few months because I was stacked. We smoked the best weed on the block. We bought top shelf liquor and went shopping for the latest shoes and clothes .Then we snuck into the Apollo and watched concerts, went bowling and hooked up with all the chicks that would normally kick us to the curb. We went out of control. Maybe you heard the saying, "It's all fun and games until someone gets hurt"? As my mother used to say and another way to put it was "A hard head makes a soft behind!" I'm here to tell you I learned the hard way and boy did it hurt.

When you start living large and choose the streets as your playground, you attract a lot of attention and not the kind you want. It all came to a head one day at the bowling alley. Cedric, Russell and I had just finished copping some weed from this guy Cowboy and his partner Dell. Dell thought he was all that and so did Cowboy with his crusty brown leather cowboy hat he used to wear all the time. And I mean "ALL THE TIME!" You would think if you're in the streets all day and night all the time, you would at least spray the thing with some Lysol or something!! Anyway we were flashing our money and I got a little bold, I told him his weed was junk dirt! I don't mean good dirt, I meant nasty crap that hurts your throat and leaves you sober. Russell and Cedric tried to shut me down thinking they would jack up their prices and jerk us but I wouldn't listen. Next thing I know I'm telling Cowboy I could get better weed and out sell him on the streets. Cowboy looks at my young behind like he wants to fight but his man Dell holds him back and asks me my name.

Out of nowhere I find myself saying, "G...G'Money!"

In my mind I was officially grown and G'Money was born. What can I say? Wouldn't you feel on top of the world being a young teenager with pockets that got the mumps and not just from Daddy's allowance but because you tapped into your GOD given talent. Girls of all colors loved me at school in the winter and camp in the summer. I was doing shows in my hood knocking the crowds out like I said earlier. I had gone back to sweep up at the Apollo Amateur night a few more times after my first win. People knew me. I was the man... or so I thought. Listen, being a man has nothing to do with money or responsibility. It has to do with life experience and that takes time to earn. Try telling that to a 15yr old that had as much as I had. No one could tell me nothing which is why I was about to get smacked down by GOD himself.

See Cowboy and Dell must have put the word out on us because by the time we got to the bowling alley that day people were watching us. Actually looking back now, the truth about that day might be a little different. I probably thought that because I had just smoked weed and was paranoid thinking I was somebody. Truth is people were most likely looking at me because I kept showing off my new clothes and flashing the big fat wad of money I had in my pocket. Cedric and Russell tried to tell me to stop and calm down but I wasn't listening to no one. I was acting like my slugger Aunt boasting my freedom or my Uncle Little Jap who knew money could buy you almost anything.

When we got to the bowling alley, Dewayne and Stacey were waiting outside to meet us. Red was already inside with his little brother Piper. The E.G. Boys and their loyalty to definitely got stronger after they saw that I kept them close even after making it big. Red's friendship was the most appreciated because he really did believe in me and gave all of his support from back even before my first James Brown concert. He was a good kid, they all were. If nothing else I could always trust them to be who they were and that was a bunch of good friends!

So as soon as we regrouped inside, we went up to the bowling alley attendant to exchange our sneakers for bowling shoes. The old man was impressed by the kicks we were wearing so we started bragging about all the shoes we had at home and flashing our money. People around us started paying attention but the only person who noticed the shift in the room was Cedric. He got us to quiet down and we went over to our lanes. We started playing and the weed started to really kick in. Next thing we were placing bets on our plays and getting loud as ever. My wad of cash stayed out collecting and getting fatter by the minute. We were laughing big and playing hard like nobody's business. As far as I was concerned the place was ours.

Next thing I know, Cedric comes over to me and says "That's right. Keep showing everybody you got money." Immediately after he said it Cedric looked to the side real stealth like.

My gaze followed his eyes and I noticed a bunch of knuckleheads grilling us hard. The weed made me panic a little especially after noticing two of the cats looked like Grip and Connie. They were known for starting beef and sticking people up. I waited a minute and as soon as I saw those two turn away for a laugh, Cedric blocked them from seeing me while I grabbed Red and dragged him into the bathroom.

At first Red had no idea what was going on. I told him about the two guys and that both Cedric and I thought they might want to do something to us.....like take our shoes. It took a minute for Red to figure out what I was trying to say. He could be so damn slow sometimes! I was starting to get frustrated with him for not catching on but I knew Red was the only one out of the E.G. Boy that I could trust with anything no matter what.

I broke it down as best as I could by saying, "Look Red, I just need a favor. There are some guys out there looking at all of us funny. One of them looks like Grip and if it is I'm sure he's going to try and rob me. Help me out here man. Take my money for me."

Red turned around and said, "What? So you want me to get robbed? Get out of here G."

This kid was comical. I couldn't believe what he just said. I tried to make myself clear, "No man. Red just take this."

Now check this out, Red took it and said, "What do you want me to do? You're telling me to put your money in "my" pocket? Are you seriously giving me your money? Thanks man! I don't know why you feel I deserve it but thanks a lot G!"

The back and forth was killing me by now and I could feel something was about to pop off. I grabbed him and said "What is wrong with you! Why are you so dense Red? Damn! I just need you to keep it for me until we get out of here o.k.? Cedric and I are pretty sure they were only scheming to do something to me. They won't bother you especially since you were here first alone with your brother. You will be safe. Take this money, put it in your pocket and just hold onto it. Give it to me when we get back to the building... home. Is that clear enough for you?"

Red still thought I was tripping for no reason but he did me the favor anyway. He made me promise to give him money if nothing went down. That felt fair so we made the exchange. Just as Red stepped into a stall to make sure the money was in a place so he couldn't lose it. At that moment, in comes Grip just like I thought he would. Right away Grip started pressuring me to gamble some money on a game. When I said no, he threatened to cut me if I didn't give him my money. I pulled out my pockets and they were empty. Grip got angry and said he was thinking about cutting me anyway. He reached towards his pocket and I cold decked him in his face. Next thing I know Red comes jumping out of the stall knocking Grip to the floor before running out of the bathroom. Now why the hell did he have to do that?! He was safe because Grip didn't know Red was in the bathroom with us. I'm telling you sometimes the kid just didn't think.

Red's Superman act put him in a position where he was now being chased down 7th avenue by a bunch of grown men thugs. Me, Stacy, Dewayne, Cedric, Russell and Red's little brother Piper tried to catch up to him. The avenue was crowded but these dudes didn't care, they kept chasing after him. I could tell Red was pretty scared because for once in his life he was moving fast as hell. We saw Red running back and forth in and out of all the people trying to loose Grip and his goons in the crowd but he couldn't shake them. Suddenly Red darts out into the street and next thing we know his body is flying through the air... Damn Red!

We got over to his body as quickly as we could. You know it's funny how some people are. As soon as he hit the pavement, Grip with his crew disappeared and so did the driver. In that moment I bet he figured he got away with murder. We were all in shock watching life slip out of Red's limp body, face filled with pain from broken ribs while his little brother cried into his chest. You always think it's going to be someone else that gets it. Guess that's what we get for playing grown before our time. Seeing Red die like that really got to me. For days after the funeral I started thinking about GOD and trying to be more righteous because things seemed to turn bad real fast. I tried to remain strong but cried about Red anyway.

Around the house, I tried talking about GOD but my Momma got really upset when I did saying to me "I don't want to hear that GOD talk around here. Here you are running around in the streets, chasing girls and smoking that weed and drinking and all that and you going to tell me about GOD? You better know GOD yourself." She almost kicked me out. If I had gotten caught with any drugs in the house my Dad would have been all over the news and scandalized for the rest of his life. You know how they twist things in the media. They could easily make it look like here is a Black man. The Deputy Chief Officer of the Fire Department and his son is dealing drugs. That was how my mother thought about it anyway. She let me know if I ever brought any of that mess into the house she would be quick to kick me to the curb and "Let the doorknob hit ya where the good lord split ya!"

I went to Ms. G about it and she told me to lay low for a while and just focus on the comedy because not only would I make people laugh, I might make myself laugh which would make me feel better. Performing in the amateur night at the Apollo had given me a way to hone my skills and develop my craft. Once again I took what I learned from that book "Think and Grow Rich" ™ and did my best to get in close with Honey Cole and Atkinson who hosted at the Apollo. After having won the amateur night so many times, they asked if I wanted to be the Master of Ceremonies. That's right... "ME"... G'Money the Master of Ceremonies for the Amateur night at the Apollo. I saw this as my first official job. It was great! Not only was I the MC, I was also asked to host comedy shows at various other venues. I hosted at Bedford Hills, club Pram, and Pegasus, which is an all-women's penitentiary. You should have seen how those women were trying to get to me the first time I hosted a show over there. I felt like the luckiest man in the history of America. They wanted me to put money in their commissary. They wanted me to get in touch with their families because I was the outside connect they had that was inside.

Like my Dad showed me, I wanted to keep moving up. I knew that Bobby Schiffman owned "The Apollo" when I first started performing there but that he had recently sold it to a man named Guy Fischer. I also knew that Fisher's right hand man Nicky Barnes used to just chill in front of the theatre during the day. I found out exactly when they were going to be there and made it a point to run into them. They were all standing out there in front of their Mercedes and wearing their big flashy gold chains. There was one guy out there I had heard about named batman that chilled with them. I spotted him because he had long pointy ears like a bat. I approached them right outside on 125th street ready to give them an unplanned audition. They must have been doing a drug deal or talking about something until I walked up on them because they seemed a little taken a back.

I approached them and they were like, "whoa, who are you?"

They looked like some really powerful men but I wasn't scared of them. I just looked them straight in the eyes and said, "Yo, my name is G-Money. I do comedy."

They started laughing at me, because these guys were murderers and killers man. It was no joke. They were nobody to mess around with!! They looked down at me and were like, "yeah right, little man... wassup?"

That was my queue. I took my chances and auditioned right outside of the Apollo Theater. I started making them laugh like it was nobody's business. My little routine had them falling over their cars they were laughing so hard!

Then one of them said, "You know what? I'm gonna find you a job man. You are going to host the show here. Come with me."

He took me inside the Apollo. Next thing I know he was giving me two tuxedos and $500 dollars! After that he took me down the block to a high end store for men! He bought me two pairs of shoes to go with the tuxedos. What really amazed me was that when it was time to pay, as soon as he reached into his pocket, the other guys in his crew stopped him and started reaching into their pockets to pay for the shoes! There were three or four guys butting heads to see who was going to pay for the shoes for him. I was blown away. This dude gave me two tuxedos, one green and one blue plus shoes to match and $500 for my pocket. I mean he just spent like $3000 dollars on me for making him laugh? Wow! Then this dude took it over the top.

He went up in the Apollo and told this guy, "Put Smokey Robinson, DJ Hollywood, and MC/ comedian G-Money on the marquee."

I was like "Damn, who the hell is this man?" Come to find out it was Guy Fischer himself! OH MY GOD! I had hit the jackpot! I couldn't believe what was happening. The rules and lessons in the book had come through for me again man. Can you imagine how good I felt seeing my name G'Money shinning bright above me in Harlem on 125th street at world famous Apollo Theatre? The surprises didn't stop there either. The first show they booked me on was with Esther Phillips, The Spinners, and Eddie Kendricks. I remember I was impersonating Eddie Kendricks that night and he came up from behind me while I was doing my set. The crowd was going crazy but I was unaware that he was behind me the whole time and that was why everyone was laughing so hard. I turned around, and oh my God, there he was.

There was such a cheese smile on my face when he gave me a big hug and said to the audience, "give this young man a hand."

Apparently he must have watched me perform before. When we officially met back in the green room after the show, he let me know that he knew about my James Brown impersonations and everything. That was the first time I experienced celebrity status. The famous Eddie Kendricks was familiar with my work before I even met him. I was speechless.

Now the night with Smokey Robinson was another trip. Smokey's organ broke down when I opened up for his show. I had to stall the audience while they fixed the organ. Since I was the opening act I was already on stage for about 45 minutes. When they told me to stay on the stage while the organ was being fixed I had to think fast. That's when I went into my bag of tricks. I started thinking about all of the voices I could do. Do you remember Felix the Cat? Well I did Felix the Cat and Rock Bottom. I did all the new stuff I had been practicing at home, experimenting with stuff I was just thinking about, cracked jokes on different audience members and before I knew it I was on stage for another 45 minutes. The show had been delayed I was actually able to entertain the crowd for over 90 minutes and everybody enjoyed me, Absolutely NOBODY left the theater! My skill was so polished that I was able to do that effortlessly without realizing it. That's what happens when you find that thing you do that GOD meant for you to love. When I went off stage to bring out Smokey Robinson, lo and behold they actually stopped the show. Smokey went out of his way to get everyone in the theatre to stand up because I had done such a good job. That was when I got my first standing ovation at the world famous Apollo Theater. In my mind I could now consider myself working as a professional comedian. Things were finally starting to get better for me.

Chapter 3

The CMB

The comedy satisfied me for a while. Ms. G was right about it making me feel better and getting my mind off of what happened to Red. My regular hang out scene and crew had changed a lot. There were a couple of guys on the comedy circuit that I became pretty good friends with like Van Paris and Rick Aviles. You might know Rick, he is a great comedian and he played a major role in the movie "Ghost™"' with Patrick Swayze and Whoopi Goldberg. When me, Rick and Van hung out we all did impersonations and it felt great to be amongst notable people of the same profession as me. They were the right people for me to be associated with, and it was great to learn from these pros. Although they were older than me, they always made me feel like we were in the same age bracket. One night, we all got together and it was a good showdown. It was so good I out showed them all! They never knew I had the knack that I possessed. I started spending so much time with my new associates, but I didn't tell my momma I was going to hang out with comedians.

My Moms was happy because as far as she knew I was staying out of trouble. The new environment and the people that I kept company with were a good look for the family. Everything was going really nice until I got jerked. Now you already know how I feel about people trying to get over on me. Here's what happened. My term came to a close at the Apollo the week before my idol James Brown opened up at the Apollo Theatre. That's right! I was replaced by my friend Rick Aviles. You know how mad I was??!! They all knew how important it was to me but like someone said, "it's only business". Not getting the chance to open for James Brown deterred me and I ended up going back to the streets despite what my mother told me. I saw how Mr. Fisher and guys like him were living and now I had to have that power and lifestyle too. I was going to be the one on top calling the shots deciding who gets cut, who gets paid and be the one making important decisions. Yeah, I was associated with all these celebrities and fat cats with nice cars and big bank accounts. I wasn't quite there yet and being let go right at that moment is what made it real clear to me. See it can be real fun and mesmerizing to be a follower hanging around taking part in all the festivities, Those guys could switch on you at any moment to remind you that it's their stuff not yours. Being a follower sometimes is good because it does have its perks. You end up being in a position where you can learn from the experiences of these other men in high positions. It gives you the opportunity to observe a leader up close in order to learn from his successes and his failures. If they like you they will tell you why they failed at certain times in their lives, why they did this or why they did that to get out of bad situations and what worked for them.

It helps you to say to yourself, "Well you know what, I'm learning from you for right now. I'll follow in your footsteps so that I can learn to become a leader myself by developing in the areas where you are strong and then add that to the strengths I already possess". You'll see in the next chapters how I became that strong leader!

You do this, all the while, remembering that your goal is not to remain being a follower. At that point in my life I only knew that the top of the ladder was being CEO or President. My young peers were mainly street-oriented and the business model you learn out there was designed to keep you in the streets or land you in jail so the fat cats could use you for slave labor. You were being paid in cigarettes and pennies on the dollar like they do today with people overseas. Ms. G and my parents taught me well and I knew better then to continue following their example. My Dad being the Deputy Chief Officer was doing well for himself and took very good care of us but he still didn't have it like some of these guys I met during my run with the Apollo. When I talked to Ms. G about it, she advised me who to look up in history and told me to study that book she gave me again. In my research I realized I wanted to be part of the 1%. People that make up the 1% in this world are some of the greatest business minds in that they have expressed their way of promotion in light that enables them to have almost complete power over the rest of the world's population that made up for the other 99%.

This 1% is made up of people that have a Mastermind mentality. The Mastermind duplicates itself so it always has at least one person it works with. Then the Mastermind plans the whole operation, analyzes every single detail and thinks it through so thoroughly that he doesn't have to execute the business himself. Just like when I went shopping with Mr. Fischer, a Mastermind's organization is able to get the job done for him and he just collects the benefits. As the mastermind, you have the power to relax or give orders and take charge of the organization that you build. You're kind of like the kingpin. As the mastermind, you're responsible for everyone in your organization and you have the ability to say whether you are a leader or a follower. As the leader, you're responsible for everyone in your organization because most people are good starters but poor finishers. As a follower, you're not responsible for anyone other than yourself and you just sit back taking notes. Point is, if you are the Mastermind you don't have someone else coming in to try to run your business. Whatever it looks like from the outside, ultimately you are in charge of your organization from how it is run to what duties the members have. Basically, you delegate who is best for the job and let them do it remembering all the time to watch and learn so you also keep getting better. This way of thinking can be applied to anything that you do. If you can imagine it, you can create it with a planned, organized structure. Everything begins with desire. A small amount of fire brings a small amount of heat. Strong desires bring strong result. Thoughts are things that are incomparable things. Thoughts are able to produce the things in your life when feeding off of Belief, Faith and Persistence. Most important of these three is the art of persistence; which is the ability of knowing that if you fail because your first plans are not sound, you just replace it with another plan until you find one that works. A quitter never wins and a winner never quits. I had the desire to do what I wanted to do. As I kept learning about people that made it into the 1%, I became more determined to master this money game and tear it up like I did so many nights at the Apollo. After all, I had become G'Money, "gonna get money, give money and make money" like the best money makers in history.

Over the next few days when I wasn't in school or working on homework, I continued to do my research and realized that whatever was going to be done has already been done. As my grandma used to say, "there is nothing new under the sun". History showed that the more money involved, the more people needed to be involved. Power of the Mastermind for me was the ability to walk in a room and say "LIGHTS OUT!" and everybody knows that it's lights out. I was learning the stories of men like John D. Rockefeller, Thomas A Edison, Napoleon Hill, Howard Hughes Cardner, the Burbanks, Woodrow Wilson, Henry Ford and Theodore Roosevelt. These were the men who succeeded and these men were not only successful but also powerful. Reading about their lives I noticed the one thing I saw that all the guys on top had in common was that they all dabbled in the street game. John Pemberton who created Coca Cola put actual cocaine in his soda which is why it became so popular that even today it's still the number one soda in the world. Whenever the Rockefellers and Rothschild's wanted to make extra money, they sold weapons to various countries for war and some say these families still do so for wars going on today. How many European and American families inherited their wealth from ancestors that stole gold, jewels and people for forced free labor from the land of the Africans and the original indigenous North and South Americans? How many museums today still make money off of relics that were robbed from ancient Egyptian tombs? What do you think would happen to you or me (G'Money) if authorities found us selling guns, selling drugs, stealing jewels off of someone's property or robbing some rich man's grave? Same thing that would happen to those men I just mentioned if there was hard evidence linking them to those crimes and they didn't have the money to pay people off. You never dirty your own hands, instead you multiply by picking people who are going to be able and willing to aide you in your business. All successful men are able to multiply themselves ten or 15 times. That enables them to be in more than one place at the same time so to avoid trouble. I bet the 1% helps maintain restrictions on society and keep certain things illegal to make it hard for competition to compete. The trick is having an organization set up where nobody knows that you're a mastermind. This is common sense man. It's absolutely necessary when your organization is involved in complicated transactions

Following the structure of building an empire and being able to duplicate myself, I figured that was the beginning of gaining the power of the Mastermind. I thought long and hard about how I could duplicate myself when I realized I already had. The E.G. Boys, my friends were loyal and trustworthy. I knew their strengths and weaknesses so it would be easy for me to pick the right jobs for them in the organization I was starting to create in my mind. First plan of action was reconnecting with them. Second, was figuring out what product we would push and how to get it. That's when I remembered the challenge Dell and Cowboy put to me just before Red died. It was unclear to me at the time if that would be the right move to make but at least I knew it was an option. The more I read, the more pieces started to fall into place for the plan developing in my Mastermind. It was time for serious action.

I was on a mission to find these guys. I went to the park, checked out every hangout spot. I went to their homes, rang their bells but nobody was home. Finally, I went up to the roof. I had forgotten how nice the view was. As

I looked around, the scenic view was amazing. It was so clear out that I was actually able to see the Empire State Building. For about 10 minutes I pictured myself owning the city! I was extremely focused that day. Suddenly, I heard a familiar sound so I looked down and there they were. Standing right outside the building on 145th street, at the corner of Malcolm X Boulevard. I ran downstairs as fast as I could because it looked like they were about to be on the move. When I caught up to them, I smiled realizing that being back on the block with the E.G. Boys felt so good. When you're with true friends, they are able to make you feel so happy and good about yourself. Real friends inspire you by making you feel wanted and appreciated. Dewayne hadn't seen me in so long, he did a double take! It looked like he had seen a ghost. Stacey turned around and when he looked at me his mouth opened wide and he looked like he was shocked to see me standing of all people standing there. Cedric just smiled, I could see the expression of excitement written all over his face. Russell tried to lie and say he had been looking all over for me. Laughing I looked around for my delayed reaction from Red before remembering things would always be different for us and it was kind of my fault. In my heart I was determined to make it up to everyone. The E.G. Boys didn't know it yet but in my mind I was getting really excited about going into business with them. If I could pull off my plan and make the capital I was aiming for, we would all be flossing back on top like before Red died. Making it big for me always included bringing my true friends along for the ride. Seeing them again reminded me how much they loved G'Money and I loved them like brothers too. Daydreaming, I could already see us as a big family like in the Godfather movies. Come to think about it now, one of my old crimey's still rolls with me up to this day almost 40 years later.

So there we all were … 15, 16 and 17 years old. By this time, hell, we had already lost one of our own to the game so our lives kind of did feel like a mobster movie. We didn't talk about it much but it was obvious that Red was missed. In that moment, I decided that no matter what, I was going to protect them and make sure we ended up as one of the top families in the street game with lots of power, money, women and connects just like the men I had researched. We shot the breeze another hour or so continuing to catch up by talking about sports, girls and wanting more money like the pimps and pushers we saw in the streets. Even though I was having a conversation with them, my Mastermind was constantly meditating on what the right next move was going to be. Finally one of my options presented itself. Russell decides that he wants to get some smoke so he hits up Cowboy who of course is with Dell. Before I even say anything, Dell asks if we could go for a walk and talk business.

He puts his arm around my shoulders and says, "What's up? Haven't seen you around in a while. Couldn't help noticing the way you were eyeing the shoes in the store down the block and my man's Mercedes across the street there. You know the only way you're getting any of those things is by becoming a stick-up kid or... doing a few things with me."

Could you believe this guy showing his balls like that? It's alright because what he didn't know was that my Mastermind orchestrated this whole meeting.

I turned to him and said, "Man you crazy. I got school and plus I don't work for nobody. I don't want to do any selling man. You're probably full of beans anyway. You ain't got nothing for me."

I had him right where I wanted. Before you know it, he was daring me to outsell Cowboy again and handing me a large brown paper bag filled with free weed! Thank GOD for my gift of gab, that move I pulled was genius. Next thing I grabbed the E.G. Boys and headed back up to the roof. After asking them to watch the bag, I headed home for a minute to get something. I'll admit, it was a little bit of a test for them. There are people you know really well but sometimes you must see how they will react under certain pressure. I needed to know if they were ready and found out that they were. When I got back from my house nothing had been touched, although they said Russell was ready to smoke up all my stuff if I had taken any longer. These guys were funny. I told them not to worry because we were definitely going to smoke some of this stuff. There we all were on top of the roof and I felt like I was standing on top of the world.

It was time to let the guys in on my plan. "Listen up; you see what I see up here? I see a city that we are about to take over. I got a serious plan but I need you guys to help me handle business and sell this stuff. If I get money, you know you get money right?! Oh and we are no longer calling ourselves the E.G. Boys because it lets everyone know where to find us. To keep the heat from coming back to the block, we're gonna call ourselves the CMB from now on: Cash Money Brothers. Is that cool with y'all?"

It's a white man's world and a white man's history/ economic book. When considering educating black men in the development of building an empire, you must keep this in perspective. Building an empire for me was like the development of a person on his way to being promoted in a business. The start of the CMB and being promoted to the position of Mastermind was like one of the keys to my success. The CMB was an attempt to duplicate myself, starting with my name. As I said earlier, you can't have a Mastermind unless there are two or more people involved in the project. The CMB stands for the "Cash Money Brothers" which works for me because my name is G-money. Get it? That's how that came about. It made it possible for me to be in five or ten places at one time. When I wasn't on the block, I could send another guy to the block.

The E.G. Boys were my main men and I was really blessed to have them by my side willing to work with me. Dewayne, Russell, Stacey and Cedric all smiled and gave me the thumbs up on the new name. Next I pulled out the bottle of Pam cooking spray I just went to my house to get.

"This is our secret weapon." I told them. "Cedric and Russell come here and block the wind. Stacey, help me lay this weed out...".

I took the cap off of the can and just before I started spraying Russell yells out, "Wait wait wait! Your momma cooks with that junk? No wonder I always be stuck in the bathroom after eating at your house. Please man; don't ruin the weed like this. At least let me smoke some first dog!"

"Shut up! You know you love my Momma's cooking. Chill out, be patient and watch the master at work. I know this is how we can make the weed stronger. My Uncle told me." My Uncle hadn't told me a damn thing and I really didn't know what I was doing but it felt right. I smacked Russell's hand out of my way and started spraying the whole bundle. The oil coated the weed really thick and it started looking all crusty, chunky and black." O.k. Russell, smoke some and tell me what you think."

"Hell NO! What!! YOU trying to kill me? You know I didn't mean what I said about your momma's cooking, damn! Look you better smoke that stuff yourself and if you die it's not my fault." Russell was looking at me like I was crazy when I snatched the rolling papers from Cedric to roll a phatty.

Then Stacey chimed in, "I don't know about this man. Look how black it is and all thick and sticky.Yeah, and it's probably going to taste like bacon. That stuff looks like poison."

We turn around and realize Piper Red's younger brother is with us giving his two cents. We probably didn't notice him because we were so used to there being 6 of us. Immediately I kicked him off of the roof. There was no way I was going to let Red's younger brother get involved in my mess. I could tell he was pretty upset the way he looked at me with such hate as he walked down the steps. I wasn't worried about it; I had to do it out of respect for Red and his mother. The street game can get pretty messy and I was not about to have another one of her kids on my conscious.

When I got to the CMB, Cedric was already smoking the joint I rolled. We passed it around and WOW was it good! In no time we ended up outselling Cowboy with my great idea to spray the weed with oil before bagging it. People would cough and it smelled like a burnt BLT so custies thought it was some hot new product. It was kind of like the war. I remember hearing my Uncle Earl talk with my Dad about how Nixon was running the country into the ground with his war and that the only way he could keep the war going was by fooling the people. Well history always repeats itself and my Uncle Earl was right about being able to fool people. When you think about it, people all over the world make their living doing just that every day. We called our "new" invention "Chunky Black". Soon our demand became greater than our supply. I mean the money was rolling in and CMB was getting bigger than ever! Yes, just like in New Jack City™ there actually was a group of teenagers called "The CMB" and it came about when the Chunky Black came about. I had my product and guys to go out there with me so I wasn't a one man team. G'Money had officially formed an alliance of a group of people that were like my brothers. There were like five of us although sometimes there were more. Everyone wasn't officially a part of the CMB, they were around but they weren't down. As time went on, I inducted about five more guys. Some worked Wall Street, some worked Staten Island, and some worked Broadway, the Bronx, Brooklyn and Far Rockaway. They were in the farthest parts of all five boroughs and set up their own operations but they were still getting the supplies from me. We even had uniforms just like in the movie. We all wore the same sweatshirt with the money sign so that people knew we were affiliated with the Cash Money Brothers.

I got tempted and seduced by material wealth and vanity when I got in the drug game by all of the influences around me. There were different influences around me from the streets to the idol figures of the world that I met through media and entertainment. All of these idol figures were loaded with the multiple Mercedes, the money and the girls. You see all these guys with the cars and the money and you want to do what they do to get the money so "I can get me a Mercedes too". That's what that saying; "Birds of a feather flock together" is all about. You really do end up living like the people you spend most of your time with. You want to be rich, hang around rich people. You want to be powerful then hang out with powerful people. I learned this in the book I was studying with Ms. G and knew that if I wanted to rule the streets, I had to look and be the part. Whatever I saw the big cats in the neighborhood doing, that's what I felt I needed to do. As a matter of fact, this one guy had the biggest medallion on his chain that I ever saw, and he was a big guy in the game. I wanted to be big like that, so I went and got me a medallion the size of a license plate so I could outrank him. It said "G-Money" in diamonds. You know what's funny and an example of the law of attraction, the first car I ever bought myself was actually a Mercedes. The big guys in the hood set the pace, and I was just following in their footsteps. Whatever they were doing, I had to do it bigger and better.

As my pockets got fatter, so did my head. I craved the applause that goes with the power so I got back strong into the comedy. Working at the Apollo opened a lot of doors for me in the entertainment business. These guys were paying me thousands of dollars to host their shows. Work was coming from all over the place because I was so well known. Even when I was working with Elmo, the Magic Christian or Scotty Flash, I was still charging them $1000 so they could put my name on their fliers: G-Money from the Apollo. It helped them fill the place up. Having G'Money on the roster meant having big money in your pockets. Of course, while I was doing these sideshows at different venues for different promoters, the negative influences were still around. At that time, if I wasn't working doing comedy, there was still the Chunky Black that we were selling when I was hanging with the crew and with the guys. I remember this one hustler who helped me get out of an altercation by selling drugs. His name was Thunderbird Johnny. I had told him that my car had been towed, and instead of giving me money to get my car back, he gave me some coke because that was all he had on him. Somehow I ended up at this lady's house and I sold everything and made enough money to get my car.

When I went back to see Thunderbird Johnny and give him the rest of the money he said, "You keep that, that's for you. But, I do want you to host this show for me!"

I said, "All right." I couldn't say no.

My family raised me right, so as I got money I gave lots of it away too. It was in my youth that I adopted the saying from the Bible, "I AM MY BROTHER'S KEEPER". Since the release of the movie, "New Jack City™", friends and acquaintances would try to be funny asking me if I was my brother's keeper. I would and still do say to this day, "Yes I am." What I meant by that is

44

back then I was responsible for putting food on a lot of people's tables. I kept money in their pockets and food on their table. I looked out for their families when they were in trouble. I was there for my friends and family and their friends and family. As Mastermind, you have to be generous in order to keep relationships with people. People never forget generosity. Life was sweet as honey with milk and I was happy to share it. Being let go by the Apollo ended up being a blessing in disguise. Hitting that low point at that time was great because necessity is the mother of invention and Chunky Black which promoted me to Mastermind came out of that. They say if you never go broke, you will never learn how to make any real money. Fast money comes and fast money goes fast, I was definitely learning how to make money come, go and come again like one of my magic tricks. Yeah, me, I chose the dark side. It was the streets and the spotlight. But I can look back today and see that I've been self-employed for over 35 years and lived like the best of them. Clearly, it was all due to seeing when to take advantage of opportunities GOD sent my way and also taking the time out for tapping into and developing the gifts GOD had given my spirit. I didn't have to want for nothing once I let GOD lead the way. Everything that I needed was provided for me and didn't lack in any areas of my life. GOD gave me the gifts and as I honed my skills I started to see all of my hidden abilities. There were so many things that I was good at, but I wanted to be the best. I had to make sure that I excelled at everything so I had to step it up.

Chapter 4

Stepping It Up

The CMB was gradually becoming one of the most popular clicks in Harlem. Mind you, I was still in high school and you couldn't tell me I wasn't FLY! Even Cowboy stopped talking snap and was buying smoke off of us. Things were just happening and I didn't always know exactly how it was working but I kept learning and expanding on my Mastermind strategies. One of the guys I liked to learn from was this kid from school Nino Brown.

Nino Brown to the world is Nino Brown. See, in the movie "New Jack City™", Hollywood depicted Nino Brown as this hard core dark skinned brother and they depicted me as the good looking light skinned brother, the pretty boy. Only the opposite was true. In real life, I fit more of the mold of the character Nino Brown played by Wesley Snipes in "New Jack City™". Even before that movie came out people used to tell me I looked like Wesley all the time. Nino was the smooth talking fair skinned pretty boy which threw some people off because it hid the fact that the kid was cold and ruthless. As he grew older, he learned how to use his swag and those good looks to prosper in the drug game.

His educational skills were limited because he hated school. My Mother knew he was no good when she met him. Of course, as a youngster I didn't know any better and wasn't paying attention to the things my mother was trying to tell me. I couldn't help it; the way Nino lived and hustled was intriguing and exciting to me. To me Nino Brown represented opportunity, another path towards the limelight. Even as kids Nino was always on the hustle. Nino's life was surrounded by various negative influences, influences that led him into the glamorous insidious lifestyles of the hustlers in New York City. He was exposed to all the shady characters of the streets and constantly came into contact with pimps, pushers, and the street hustlers. Some say it was because of all this that the real Nino Brown had a moneymaking skill that would blow your mind. Nino knew how to get money, lots of money. A day with Nino was almost certain to put some cash in your pocket. Whether it was rigging washing machines to get free washes, or placing his arm up a soda machine and pulling down free sodas. From an early age Nino had a hustle! One time Nino, me and a couple other kids hopped the train downtown and hit every gum machine from 96th street train station to Wall Street. When we got back to Harlem we had shopping bags filled with gum and candy. That's how life was for us. Just like me he always wore the hippest clothes but he never paid retail prices. He was a real New Yorker that knew how to bargain and bought his merchandise from the best of the boosters in the city. We were always hype and looking for the next scheme or hustle and Nino never let me down. He had a mind-set that would make you curious about how he knew how to make money so well. Later, I discovered Nino decided at an early age that he wanted to be a kingpin. It all starts with that desire. We both had our hustle and we were both young and flossing like Fat Catz in Harlem. Lo and behold, Nino always had a way of showing you there was an easier way to live and Nino always had the gift of showing the negative influence of things in a positive light. We influenced each other and grew up like brothers, sharing ideas plans and a lifestyle of fame and riches in the streets of New York and other various cities. If you saw me, you knew Nino was not far behind. Nino and I had each other's backs.

Hiding my secret life from my parents started getting hard when comedy, the hustle and my other extra-curricular activities began wearing me down. It was becoming difficult to wake up on time for school especially since most of the time I was pretending to wake up having just snuck in from the night before. People all over New York City knew about Chunky Black and they wanted it all day and night. People needed to be added to the CMB in order to take care of our customers. More members meant I had to step up my Mastermind game and make more money to support the team because right then I just couldn't afford the expansion. I became a bit on edge, we all did. The guys tried to relax by coming to my comedy shows but nothing beats sleep and we were just not getting it. Cedric and Russle started getting into stupid arguments over nothing. Righteous Dewayne tried to keep things cool between us but you could tell he was stressed like an old man trying to please a young, feisty hooker. I mean he looked old before but now his face was looking even more like a mummy's dust fart. Stacey kept acting nervy. It all was getting a little bit intense.

People knew to stay out of my way because I was ready to beat up anybody over the dumbest reasons. I remember one day finding out someone my age was hustling Red's little brother Piper and his young friends. Piper had searched this dude out but that didn't matter, I still went all the way up to the

Bronx by myself to find the guy, grabbed him by his Afro in front of his friends and went Thai Bo on his face. Some called me Scarface because that's just how I was acting... high, overzealous and looking to scar up somebody's face. My Mom's figured my bad behavior was due to me hanging out with Nino Brown. My mother couldn't stand Nino because Nino didn't have any manners and he was disrespectful towards my mother. One time Nino cursed my mother out.

He came to my house, my mother told him I couldn't come outside and Nino said, "Well Flubber you Mrs. G-Money."

My mother said, "Oh no, you WON'T talk to me like that, and you WON'T be with my son!"

I tried to come to Nino's defense because he was like my best friend now but that just made things worse. A lot of the time I was smoked out so I couldn't see what was really wrong with that picture. If anyone tried to disrespect my mother or anyone else in my family today, they would be cut off in more ways than one. But back then, all I felt was the pressure coming from all angles. In order to protect my sanity, I hardened myself because cracking up wasn't an option that I was willing to explore.

All day long in school, and all through our nights of hustling, the CMB kept trying to find a way to bring in more capital. Somehow we needed to get more supply so we could service more people which meant more money. More money would help grow our business to where we could add more employees to help free up our time so we could rest and relieve this tension from work. Then one night after a comedy show, Stacey came up to Dewayne, Russell, Cedric and I while we were in the middle of a joint to tell us that Dell had been arrested. This was just the break we needed! I explained to the CMB that, if Dell had been taken off of the streets that meant whoever was supplying Dell will need a new head runner. Since I was Dell's best hustler, I was probably next in line to meet Dell's connect. Turns out I was right.

My first day meeting Susan I will never forget. When the CMB first heard the name, we all thought it must be this hot, Queen Bee, Foxy Brown looking kind of chick. Now Dewayne and Russell were missing in action that night so it was just me, Cedric and Stacey. We came with guns and everything just in case. Oh snap! That's right, forgot to tell you about what happened to Russell and why he was laying low! Well, he was selling up in the Bronx and everything was going smooth. His custy handed him money and he gave the kid some weed in exchange. Russell leaves and stops somewhere to take a leak before heading back into Manhattan. Just as he starts taking a piss, Russell gets smacked in the back of his head with something hard. He looks up and there's his last customer leaning over the top of the next stall with a gun to Russell's head demanding the rest of the drugs. Russell hands over his duffle bag filled with weed. He is just happy to get away with his life. He says the customer ended up giving the duffle bag back empty because Russell had pissed on it during the commotion! Knowing Russell, yeah it's possible he just smoked all that. Still, since he seemed pretty shaken, had a lump on the back of his head and the bag smelled like piss, we all gave him the benefit of the doubt!

Besides, lately it seemed a lot of the clients we ran into had a tendency to show their balls, acting like they want to do something. The Russell incident was the last straw. Cedric hung out with his mother's boyfriend a lot who owned a club and had a lot of connects. One of the connects had a son that Cedric became good friends with. The kid sent us to this watermelon truck that used to park uptown right off the Westside highway. They sold a lot of fruit but if you knew the right password they would sell you a melon packed with hardware. We didn't want people messing with us or our product so we figured this was the next step in our growing empire.

Anyway, I don't know where Dewayne was the night we met Susan but that's why Russell wasn't there and how we got our hands on some guns. So we were ready but I wanted to stake the place out alone first. It was a bold move but I felt it best to tell Cedric and Stacey to wait for me at the deli where they were hidden but could still see where I was going. As I approached the building I had been to for my meeting with Susan, I felt a little nervous because this seemed like big time for me. When I got to the front of the place there was this heavyset, hairy bear looking man sitting on the stoop. He asked me who I was and who I was looking for so I told him. Next thing I know I'm following this big, ugly dude up to the second floor with Stacey and Cedric waiting for me down the block. The man goes up to this door, does a funny knock, it opens and we walk into a one bedroom apartment. I remember thinking to myself that I needed a place like that for the CMB as the door quietly closed shut behind me. The big guy leads me into a back room with a desk. He closes that door too and sits down sizing me up. Now I'm freaking out wondering where Susan is and maybe I shouldn't have come up here alone. Damn!

Finally he breaks the silence and says, "What do you want kid?"

"I'm G'Money and Susan sent for me to come talk about some business. What do you mean what do I want? If she didn't tell you, maybe you're not supposed to know." I said this as hard and as cool as I could because the last thing I needed was this guy knowing I felt a little intimidated by him.

In a deep, menacing tone he shoots back, "Listen I don't care who you are punk! All you need to know is that whatever happens to my stuff is your responsibility. Got it?" He starts laughing and smirks, "You look like the type of little dude that likes running shit. You think you got this game all figured out don't you? You think you got it all on lock?"

Gunshots are fired outside and my heart stops. 5 seconds later there's that funny knock again at the door. Me and the Bear dude run into the main room while the other guys in the apartment look through the peek hole and open the door.

In rushes this scared looking guy over to the dude I was talking to saying, "I'm sorry Susan, they caught me off guard!"

Turns out that "Susan" was this guy's alias to keep the cops off of his scent!

Then, in comes Cedric and Stacey busting in through the front door right after, drawn and fanning the room yelling, "Where is G'Money! Yo G you o.k.!? Where are you?!"

Once Susan and I realize what's going on, we calm everyone down and Susan gives me the heads up that I'm alright. He then motions for some of his guys to put together a pound for me. While they do that, Susan uses a hammer to smash up the fingers of the man that let Cedric and Stacey into the building. We could tell he was doing it in front of us so that we would know he ain't no joke. As soon as the pound was packed and ready to go, we were happy to get out of there.

Although the three of us still couldn't find Dewayne, the three of us met up with Russell and congregated at our favorite spot on the roof. It was where we started the CMB and it was where we were gonna start making history.

It was my job to hype these guys up because I wanted to get Susan his money back as quickly as possible. "O.K. CMB, this is our chance to start making some real money. Y'all ready? I got the cooking spray... Let's show them what Cash Money Brothers is all about!"

Man when I say we were on point with our game, I mean we were moving like a well-oiled machine! I sprayed, Stacey and Russell put the weed into little envelopes and Cedric bundled them together and packed the shoulder bags. We had this thing running like clockwork. The cops tried to catch us but we were too smooth the way we watched each other's backs and exchanged products between us whenever they did catch and search us. Each of us had taken a quarter and we had Susan's $1600 dollars by that night. When I delivered the money to him he was so happy. Not only did I give him the $1600 dollars he asked for, I sold the pound at three quarter its weight so he got an extra $400 dollars on top of that. Susan doubled my supply in exchange for me tripling his profits.

It was just what CMB needed. Our empire had grown and now we employed over 20 people. Some worked Wall Street, some worked Staten Island, and some worked Broadway, the Bronx, Brooklyn, and Far Rockaway. They were in the farthest parts of all five boroughs and set up their own operations, but they were still getting the supplies from me. The CMB was now officially making at least 6 figures a week. The money bought us the man power needed to give us some free time. Right away I put money down on a place up in the Bronx where we could take care of some of our business and chill. Stacey and Dewayne focused a bit more on their school work. Russell would disappear then come back around and tell us stuff like he was vacationing in Paris and headed back to Japan for two months. The stories this guy came up with were crazy but it was Russell so you never knew if it was real or not. Cedric started working for his mom's boyfriend. All he had to do was watch the man's top of the line cars while the dude ran errands. Cedric got $100 dollars a stop, easy money. Sometimes I would go sit with him especially if it was early during a weekday. I really wasn't feeling what they were trying to teach me in school.

At that time, I would cut school a lot because my Dad wasn't home which made it easy to get away with stuff that I did. Everyone thought I was doing so well with school and being a big time celebrity comedian so he felt o.k. traveling back and forth to the Dominican Republic securing a house and land for the family. Little did my parents know that between the knowledge I was getting out of the books recommended by Ms. G and the money I was making in the streets and on stage, I didn't see the point in going to school. It was all smooth sailing until my Mom came home really early from work one day and found me discarding an absence notice letter that had come from my school.

To make things worse, when my little brother got back that afternoon from school he ratted on me and showed her where I was keeping money in the house. I think I had about four thousand dollars stashed in a shoe box at my mom's crib. I couldn't believe my own brother ratted me out about the money when the only reason he knew I had the money was because I wanted to look out for him and the family whenever they needed money. Dad did tell me to take care of everyone while he was gone.

Turns out he had asked my mom's for some to get something and she told him she didn't have it so he flipped and opened his fat mouth. Great timing! I wish he had just asked me, damn! When my mom's confronted me about keeping money in the house I panicked and said it was Nino Brown's money. She hit the ceiling. She told me to get the money out her house because she'd be damned if I jeopardize my Father's job or her reputation behind what some lil' no good Negro gave me to hold and she was quick to kick me out. You know, "let the doorknob hit ya where the good Lord split ya". Overnight, I was packed and sent to live with my Uncle Earl while Father was out of town. With all the potential I had to be a great performer, I was still a kid and kids at times gravitate toward trouble. This was my Mother's attempt to get me as far away as possible from trouble and troublemakers like Nino Brown. Her plan worked or at least it slowed my street game down for a while. Maybe that was for the best, you know GOD works in mysterious ways!

My Uncle Earl's first wife was a deputy warden in one of the prisons in New York. Just like my Dad, Uncle Earl was also a high official in the City of New York. My Mom's was right to send me to him because all in all he was a good role model for me. You know how it is when you live with someone that looks just like you, is doing well and gets lots of respect? It sometimes helps build up your own confidence. My uncle and I favored each other. Many times I'd be walking down the street and be mistaken for my uncle. Imagine how I felt walking down the street and people thinking that I was one of those high end officials working for the city of New York. Being given that kind of respect felt good, even if it was only for a short time. Uncle Earl had been in the Army, gone to Vietnam and he didn't play. My uncle was strict but he was more like a big brother to me.

He'd simply say, "If you mess up you're gonna get tapped." My uncle was a no-nonsense kind of guy. He knew what I was up to. We bumped heads a lot especially when it came to me taking his car.

When I went to stay with my uncle he had just gotten married to a new, young wife who was very pretty. I was still a little rebellious, so when my uncle wasn't around my cousin and I wouldn't listen to her. Who was she to tell us what to do when she just a tad bit older than us? Plenty of days she'd call my uncle at work crying. You see, I was G'Money and this new chick was a control freak. Getting in trouble night after night because this young bride would tell on us going out was getting a bit crazy. After staying with my uncle for a while, I got a job, saved my money and moved out. I rented a room and as a young kid still in high school, I was living on my own. I was doing well.

When I got around to it, I told the CMB that I had my own place and one day Nino showed up at my room. Being the young, naive kid that I sometimes was, I wanted to impress him. Although I was living in a room that I shared the kitchen and bathroom, I showed Nino the place like I was taking him on a tour of a five-bedroom mansion. I excitedly told him how I could bring girls over and have them spend the night and that brought a chuckle outta him. Hell, Nino had girls spending the night with him at his mother house for the longest. It was nothing to go by Nino's house to pick him up and he'd have a girl hiding under the sheet of his bed!

As we were standing in my room Nino says, "Let's get outta here, I'm feeling closed in". I asked him where he wanted to go. He says, "Let's go up to see Donna and Rhonda," (two girls we knew from the Bronx) and take them to the movies."

I said to him, "Man, I don't have any money for that." I'll never forget what happened next. Nino reached down in his pocket and gave me $240.00 dollars in cash.

He said, "Here... take that; now let's go."

I said, "Man, I don't have anything to wear!"

Nino said, "Come down stairs." When we reached the bottom of the stairs, there was a limo parked by the curb. Nino moved toward the limo and motioned me over. I was in amazement, and almost disbelief.

I said, "Man... whose limo is that?"

He simply said "Ours." You can't imagine the excitement that was building inside me. I asked how long we have this for to which he answered, "All day."

I was like WHOA. Nino then told the driver to open the trunk. Nino reaches inside the trunk and pulls out brand new clothes and sneakers. He hands them to me and tells me to go upstairs and get dressed. This would become the typical Nino, always flush with cash and not afraid to share his wealth with friends. Needless to say by now the limo parked outside my room began to draw attention and finally a crowd gathered around trying to learn what famous person was in their neighborhood. When I got dressed and came back downstairs I felt like a superstar again. The girls who never paid me any mind were now all standing in awe as if they suddenly realized I was the man of their dreams and I loved the attention! Nino was used to it so it didn't faze him one way or another. He had the looks and the personality that made it in a guy's best interest not to leave his girlfriend alone in the presence of Nino Brown.

We jumped in the car and headed to the Bronx to pick up the girls. These were the two prettiest Latina honeys you could ever imagine. They were FINE! We took them out to the movies, grabbed a bite to eat and it was during this time while taking them back home that Nino and his date got into an argument. When we got back to the Bronx, Nino and the girl were still going at it. By the time the limo had pulled up on the girls' block and we got out of the limo, Nino had punched the girl in the face. I tell you the kid was cold hearted! All that was running through my head was Maaaan... what did he do that for? The girl started yelling in Spanish and it looked like every Spanish guy in the Bronx came out to help this girl. Next thing I know I see Nino take off running and a herd of Spanish dudes took after him. A group of Latino guys confronted me but my date told them I was cool so they left us alone. All I kept thinking about on the Limo ride back home was, if those guys caught up to Nino it was over for him. When I saw Nino later, he said he had jumped in a cab and gotten away. I went to hand Nino back the roll of cash left from what Nino gave me earlier. He told me to keep it and so I used the money to redecorate my room. I bought a new stereo, all of the new R&B sounds I could find, some bed linens and some curtains. My room was now plush just like at Momma's house.

Contrary to the movie "New Jack City™", it was around this time that Nino Brown introduced me to the dope game. Before that I knew nothing about it, I was strictly "Chunky Black" green. Not long after that incident in the Bronx, I began feeling the need to make some real money again. I asked Nino how he was getting all this money. To me, it seemed as if he always had an endless amount of cash. He said come with me downtown and you just stand there with me and when I tell you to hand me one you hand me one.

Naive as I was I asked, "Hand you one of what?"

He answered "Of this stuff here" as he handed me a bag. He then went and explained to me that it was dope and that the people really come out for this stuff. Never get caught holding the brown bag. It was kind of like another way of saying; the Mastermind should always keep his hands clean. This is the best advice I could ever share with you.

So we get downtown and Nino took me into this house on 129th Street and 8th Avenue in Harlem. I was to pass him packets of dope through the peephole when he requested it and in the amounts requested. In less than an hour Nino knocked on the door telling me to pass out X-amount of packets of dope. He then gave me the money for the drugs and I then passed him what he wanted. We were done!

He knocked on the door and said, "Yo man... how many you got?" I told him we were out, finished. Like Mission Impossible, Nino always had an exit strategy. "Okay," he says. "I'm going to catch a cab and when you hear me signal "A-O-K-O", this means I want you to come outside and get in the cab.

When I got the signal, I hurried and left the building and jumped in the cab. Mind you, both my pockets are bulging with cash. My pockets had a serious case of the mumps baby! It was mind boggling the amount of money Nino made and gave away. He told me to keep all the ones and fives and just give him the tens, twenties and fifties. I swear it was like, darn.. this dude didn't have to be smart because what he lacked in book smarts he made it up in his ability to make money. I mean isn't the point of going to school to learn a trade that will make you money to live off of? Well I didn't know any working class man or woman making money like my high school friend was on his spare time. You know I wanted to learn more about this stuff. The third day I came by Nino's crib he wanted to take the day off, said he was tired and wasn't going out.

I was thinking about the cash I wouldn't be making that day so I said, "Awe come on man... Look man, I'll go out there by myself. You know you can trust me." He said o.k. and gave me dope. I got a cab, picked up one of my friends Ronnie, a new member from the CMB, and we went out on the block. As soon as I hit the block and told a few people I got it, the junkies lined up to get some of the dope I had. Now just like Nino did me, I sent Ronnie into the building and I'm outside serving the junkies. The power I felt being out there with the dope was intoxicating. Imagine this young high school kid telling grown ass men "'back the hell up or I ain't serving nobody". Well...everybody listened! I was Nino's man and now I was making Ronnie my man out there.

That first time me and Ronnie went out there everything was cool. I bought Nino back the money and he gave me my cut. The second time me and Ronnie went out on the block, the police came and Ronnie threw all the bundles of dope in the air! Next thing I seen all the dope fiends made a mad dash picking up the drugs. Because of what Ronnie did we never got caught with the drugs, but now I owed Nino Brown's cold ass a lot of money. I'm in the hole $3,000 dollars. I convince Ronnie to go stick up somebody with me to get this money back. We set out looking for something to stick up like a Jack in the Box or McDonald's. Ronnie got hyped, said he'd do the actual stick up but wasn't doing nothing unless he got to carry the real gun. Since we didn't have our regular supplies like we did in Esplanade Gardens, we had one real gun and one fake gun. Things got tight because we couldn't find nothing open and nobody to stick up. Just as we were about to go home and call it a night some, dudes came out of nowhere yelling, "Smoke, smoke, got that smoke..."

Smiling, me and Ronnie looked at each other and we couldn't believe it. We had spent all night looking for someone or something to rob and this dude walk right in to our desperate need to get some green. We ask the dude if he can get us a pound of weed.

The dumb ass says, "Yeah mon, wait 'ere."

We tell him we're waiting in the building because it's cold. There was like four guys in the building. We waited until the guy comes back downstairs.

The Rasta says, "Come mon... come mon!" and we get on the elevator with like eight other guys. The door closes and the guy starts saying, "You not playing wit' us mon? You not playing wit' us mon? You wan' da smoke right mon?"

We said" yeah", so the guy opens the bag to show us the smoke. Next thing I Know, Ronnie's gun is out and I pull out the fake gun. We start screaming and yelling telling all the suckers to get on the ground. We made them take off all their clothes after we got the weed. We got all their clothes, ran down one flight of stairs, slammed the door, went down a different flight of stairs and then I threw all the clothes out on another floor. We had these Rasta's butt naked and I didn't want them chasing after us. Messing around I had to leave Ronnie there. He was going over board, started rummaging through all their pockets when I left. By the time Ronnie caught up with me I had already caught a cab and was getting in so I could get my behind home. I tried to get the driver to hurry up and go because I really wasn't waiting for Ronnie but he made it in the cab anyway. The cab driver was trying to get us to pay him before he started driving and here we are trying to get away from the scene? Too bad for the cabbie Ronnie had the real gun so we point the gun at driver from behind the partition and told him to drive. We take him to some dark neighborhood, tell him to stop and pullover then we wound up robbing the cab driver for $90 dollars. After kicking the cab driver out into the street like Grand Theft Auto, since Ronnie couldn't drive I wound up driving the car back to Manhattan. It took us about ten to fifteen minutes. When I got back to

Nino all I had for him was a pound of weed and six hundred dollars. I told Nino everything that happened and why he was now short $1400 dollars.

Can you believe this dude laughed at me and was like, "Oh that's all right, don't worry about it."

Dumbfounded, I'm sitting there saying to myself, after all that mess I'd been through that night, he's gonna laugh at me and say, 'don't worry about it…it's alright?". Like I didn't just put my life on the line over $3000 dollars that he obviously didn't care too much about. I mean I could have been the one left naked in some strange hallway. Damn, what was I missing? Anyway I learned my lesson that night and I started making money with Nino. When I felt I was finally ready again and wanted to do my own thing too, Nino offered me a deal.

Nino was selling bundles of dope but he also had quarters of dope for sale. He offered me $15 dollars a quarter where quarters were for $65 dollars on the streets. He didn't let me in on what money he was making as well but I'm sure if he was giving it to me at $15 dollars a quarter, he was probably getting it at $7 dollars a quarter. Nino wouldn't do it unless the mathematics was right. This new venture helped me step my game up. One of my guys was selling 500 quarters a day and he was consistent. The dope business had gotten real good for me. Both Nino and I were getting serious paper in the drug game at an early age. Mind you we were both still in high school. We were balling so hard we'd take limos to school and have them on hold while we were in class. Things were really popping off but not like they could have been if I was still living in Esplanade Gardens. Where I was staying was too far away from everything to put the time in that I used to. I just wasn't there.

My mother sending me to stay with my uncle probably saved me from being a part of many tragic accidents that seemed to happen in Harlem all the time back then. Actually, I know now it was for the best. Before my mother kicked me out I always kept a low key and always moved as if the Feds was watching me even though I never killed anybody. I did my share of beating up people, but I have never killed anybody. We had respect for mothers and besides, death seemed like letting someone off too easy. I preferred letting them live with the shame that they got punked by the CMB for stepping out of line. Well you ever heard that saying, "Live by the gun, die by the gun?" Soon after we got the guns from the watermelon man, Dewayne stepped out of the game. He ended up getting a scholarship to some Ivy League school. When I moved away, Russell and Stacey also fell back and got back into their schoolwork. Cedric kept things going but ran into complications with some old beef we had and ended up with a jammed gun at a playground shoot out. When the gun finally did go off, Cedric ended up shooting his friend Kevin in the stomach. Kevin dies and Cedric was shipped up the river. Nino was also accused of an accidental homicide, one of our best friends. Apparently Nino was playing with a gun, it went off and killed the boy. Nino ended up in jail for that.

I found most of this stuff out one day when my Father returned to New York and came looking for me unannounced. It was cool though, we went shopping and talked. My Mother had been right but that is exactly what pushed me to be more to the elements of the street life. Most kids when you tell them no, they will go out of their way to discover why not for themselves. Curiosity makes kids eager to know all of the things that you tell them not to do. And at the time when your parents are forbidding you to do something or hang out with a certain crowd, you don't realize it's for your own good. You don't see the same views that your parents see when you're a kid. All that you know is that you want to have a good time.

Having too much of a good time, without caution, can lead you down a deadly path. If I would have known what I know now, I would have thought twice about walking down the path I walked as a kid. There are so many things I had to discover on my own, because I let uncles, cousins and everything that I was exposed to dictate my thinking and the way I lived.

Everyone around me incorporated their way of thinking and living into my life and I followed behind them, but I needed structure and the proper teachings. Although they were teaching me, the things they applied to my teachings was not always correct in the light of GOD, because I was learning how to live in sin.

My Dad was concerned but he understood what I was going through when he left for the Dominican Republic leaving me the man of the house. My conversation with my Dad's was getting really deep while we were popping in and out stores. Suddenly, I caught on to how much summer clothes and shoes he was buying me. When I asked why, he told me my mother, brother and sister missed me and we were going to see them. Apparently everyone had moved out of Manhattan except for me! At first I had no idea what my father was getting at and the whole thing seemed very confusing. Can you feel me? Think about it... G'Money had never left the state of New York and now without any notice G'Money was getting into an airplane that was on its way to the Dominican Republic! WOW!... talk about surprise visits!

Chapter 5

Tropical Paradise

When I stepped off of that plane in Santo Domingo, Oh My GOD it was like Heaven! The sun hit me in my eyes, I was blind and I knew my Father had abducted me! I was exiting the Mother Ship! Oh but let me tell you, when my vision finally refocused and I saw where I was... GOD Damn! I have never seen anything so hot and breathtakingly beautiful in my life! I swear the Dominican Republic is the utopian of paradise. Imagine little black me walking into that having only seen the city streets of New York and some raccoons and squirrels upstate in a Christmas tree. The palm trees, the salt water breeze, I was carried away by its magnificence. You haven't lived until you've been to the Caribbean.

The ride to the house was unbelievable. I saw the most mesmerizing women...and the view of the beach was amazing...the crystal clear water was magnetizing...I was speechless because it all seemed surreal. My Dad gave me a tour of all his favorite spots. He showed me around and took me to see all of the main attractions; it was so much to see. I was tired but I didn't want to miss a thing so my eyes stayed open.

Eventually the car pulled into the driveway of our new house. It was unbelievable; my Dad had bought a house that looked like something from a movie. It looked like one of those beautiful homes you see in a magazine or some type of resort that would be in a travel brochure.

We each had our own rooms. My brother's room was the size of two bedrooms. My sisters room was huge...when I walked in I just looked all around and was like, "Wow, look at all of this. She tried to keep me out but I wanted to see every inch of what my Dad got us. My parent's room was like the size of two master's bedrooms. Talk about a master's bedroom. They had their own bathroom included in their bedroom, and it was so huge, it was like an extra bedroom. My room was hotness too. It had twice the amount of space of my sibling's room. It was like a dream. I walked around my room, felt the bed which was so plush and made from the finest materials that I felt like a King. My Mother came in to see me after a while and gave me a really big hug. She was so glad to see me still alive. We talked about so many things that day, and she expressed how much I meant to her. And I was just happy to be back with my family again. I was content!

Then she asked me if I had a chance to see my view. "I got a view?" I thought to myself. She led me over to the window opposite my bed and I looked out. Amazing! The land my Father bought was a lot of acres. We had goats, chickens, and horses. The trees were even more beautiful than the palm trees at the airport. We had a Guava tree, passion fruit tree, papaya, and mango.

This was much better than the place I had in the Bronx. We even had helpers. Until then, I thought only white people did that kind of stuff. The women were all nice and dark like me and so beautiful. Dinner that night was out of this world. We ate the type of food that belongs in a five star restaurant. Before I got on that plane earlier that day I thought I was going to hell, but I'm here to tell you that the Dominican Republic was nothing short of a tropical paradise.

When I woke up the next day my parents had company over. That was the day I met my friend Ricardo. Ricardo was there to help my family out when they first moved because they didn't speak any Spanish. He was a very decent guy. He was almost like a brother in the family. Ricardo was also a smart guy. He worked at a hotel for American tourists. They would give him American money to pay for their hotels and he would go and exchange the money into pesos and pay for their hotel in pesos and keep the difference. He would make a whole lot of money doing that. Here I was flipping drugs for $200 dollars a pop tops and this guy was flipping hotels at $20,000 dollars a pop minimum! This was definitely the kind of guy I knew I needed to hang out with; a man that's smart with money and knows how to have a good time.

Ricardo and I started hanging out on a regular basis. Usually, during the day we would take a ride into town and he took me with him sometimes when he went to work. He taught me a little about his business and I would help out by assisting him and running errands for him. Ricardo really took to hearing about what I learned out of my favorite books like "Think and Grow Rich™". I learned some valuable lessons from him and he learned a few things from me too. Ricardo taught me the ropes of things, and life in DR was sweet. One day Ricardo took me for a ride to some of the other towns and he showed me some places that his friends and him use to go to have a good time. It was a great experience.

My parents trusted Ricardo because he helped them out and it seemed like he was a nice hard working guy that liked staying out of trouble. This was great because it gave me the freedom to spend as much time as I wanted learning about his lifestyle, how he maintained it and how he ran his business endeavors. At night Ricardo made sure to take me to the hottest clubs on this side of the island. This was the time when he made most of his money deals. You should see the parties and beautiful women they have there. I remember this one night we were surrounded by a whole bunch of women who were fighting for our attention, and guys were just looking at us wishing they had it like that. Business was going smoothly, my pockets were swollen and I was living the life. I literally felt I was living out Scarface, living in the big house, driving the nice cars, making business deals, doing it in the clubs, coke and all. Man I knew I could live like this forever.

I ended up staying in the Dominican Republic for over 2 years. Life was so perfect and serene there I really didn't want to go back to the United States. My parents had to sit me down and explain that they wanted me to make something of myself. Dollars were more valuable than pesos, so if I wanted something out of life it was best if I earned my money in money making Manhattan. It's always best to work smart over working hard. After all, I could always visit and use my American dollars to live like a king whenever I decided to travel back to see them. If I worked in D.R., I'd get paid more than 50% less than what I would for the same job in New York. Once they made that clear I realized staying was just plain stupid, almost as stupid as flirting with death and incarceration like I did as a kid. Luckily the Dominican Republic and my experiences in the Caribbean heat sweat that right out of me! I was in my early 20's now and was ready to get a good job, save and get something nice like my Dad had done. Yeah I still dreamed big but now I also wanted to do it big the right way. Just before I left to go to the plane that went back to New York City, I gave Ricardo all of my clothes. We were the same size and I felt after all he had done for me it was the least I could do.

I said "Look man, you can have this, you can have that, and you can have all of that because where I'm going its cold!" It's a good thing I did that because good things and generosity always comes back to you when you need it most.

Chapter 6

Back on the Grind

When I got back to New York, the first thing I realized was how dirty everything was. If the Dominican Republic was heaven, this was definitely Hell's Kitchen. Since almost all of my family was still out of the United States, the only place I had to go was my Cousin Booby's place. At that time, I was staying with him in his one room and figured out quick that I needed a way to get me some money.

As soon as I arrived, after we said our hellos and he helped me with my bags, the first thing my cousin says to me is, "Yo man you gotta pay me some rent."

Just like that? Really? I looked at him and said, "I just got here...are you serious man? I don't have a problem paying you rent, but you know I ain't got no money."

He looked at me hard saying, "Well, you better go down to the welfare center and get some food stamps or something." My cousin was a nice guy. He was probably just insensitive towards my loss of fortune due to how I treated him as a kid. Definitely, there was no spoiling going on in here anytime soon. I could understand where he was coming from not wanting a grown man living in his apartment that's not paying his own way family or not.

That night as I lay on my cot breathing the city's smoggy air, I concentrated on turning my mind back into the money making machine that ruled this town 2 years prior. I understood that something inside me wanted the chance to build myself back up again which is why I was in this broke position. My Mastermind was beginning to awaken, lessons came back to me. I meditated on how the thoughts you think have the power to produce the physical things you have in your life. See the brain receives and broadcasts what it hears. You learn that as a young man. That's learning how to remember things, but also hearing the right things that can program your mind to think positive so that you draw to yourself the things you want. By the time I went to bed I had a plan and I knew what to do.

That next morning I got up at 5am, showered, had some breakfast and went straight down to the welfare office like my cousin told me to. Even though I was one of the first ones there, I wasn't seen 'till 2pm. The whole experience got me so discouraged. They asked me about my momma. They asked me about my momma's momma. They wanted proof of all this stuff. I was lying to them anyhow, but man you know what? All day long I waited to be seen and when I saw the case worker she was talking about I gotta bring her this and I gotta bring her that? They couldn't tell us this crap while I was standing on line all morning? Seriously, I started getting frustrated! I waited in this dingy, nasty smelling place where the halls smell likes piss and they have nerve to give me attitude when they're getting paid obviously to waste my freaking time!? I mean this was ridiculous! People come here because they need help and this is the stuff they do to you? Cursing everyone out, I broke out of that center and decided to hit up the pavement to see what jobs were out there.

By the end of the day I had managed to land a job with this Jewish man on 75th street. He needed sales people to push his cleaning products and figured since I was black; I'd be able to carve out a profitable market for him in the projects. When I showed up to work the next day it was me, this other brother and a couple of white guys. Of course he assigned the brother and me to Harlem and the white boys to all the rich neighborhoods. There was no offence taken, because over the years I learned that with Jews it's not about black or white, it's about green. He told us to go where he thought we would make more money for him. As for the white boys, I could tell they were looking at it like a race thing. Thought they had one up on me because theoretically their clients had more money than mine. Little did they know they were messing with G'Money. The Jew was paying us off of commission and I wasn't about to let any one of those racist guys outsell me.

As soon as I got my supplies to sell, the first thing I did was run to Esplanade Gardens. What my Mastermind needed right now was the CMB team to blow these guys out of the water. I started asking questions to find out who was around. Next thing I know I'm being felt up by cops. Thank GOD I had gone straight because the same guys that used to be late night on the beat were now sitting in detective seats and they knew my face. Told me they couldn't wait to throw me in jail with Cedric. I was hot but the streets were hotter than ever. This was the year before elections so the politicians that put the drugs out there as traps were now reeling it all in especially in Harlem. They gave me a threatening warning that reminded me why I should keep a low profile from now on.

Eventually I ran into Stacey, Dewayne and Russell. Man I was so happy to see them! Dewayne had majored in Criminal Law and was almost finished school. Stacey was still dancing and a smooth operator. Russell, well he was trying to tell me some long over exaggerated story, and I just started shaking my head... but you know about Russell. We agreed to meet up on the roof in 15 minutes which gave me time to get my supplies and a bucket. When I returned back up there the view really stuck out to me and I knew it was only up from here. My vision felt promising, the science was right on, the CMB was back together and the Mastermind was at work again. I took my time opening the cleaning supply bottled and emptied their contents into the bucket.

As I'm working my magic I hear Stacy arrive and say, "Oh SNAP! G'Money is back with a new formula. Yeah."

Then Russell yells, "Hell no! I'm definitely not smoking that! What's wrong with you G?"

It took a minute but eventually the CMB realized the product we would be pushing wasn't drugs but Brookshire Cleaning Products. Stacey was right about one thing, we were going to reuse the Chunky Black business formula to do it. These principles and laws have been applied again and again in order to operate and organize the CMB and it work with anything. I figured out a way to stretch the cleaning product to where it still worked but we got more supplies to sell. More supplies meant more money. Dewayne was down, eager to learn from my make shift business school. Stacey ended up helping out but he was annoyed because he felt there was more money in the drug game. After I reminded him about Cedric and Red he stopped his complaining and agreed to give it a whole hearted try. Russell came along laughing the whole time because he knew if nothing else he would get some good stories out of this experience. Our machine started working, just like I thought we were tearing it up overnight and the Jew was loving it! Let me tell you he was not the only one. It was with this job that I learned just how much women get turned on by a business man in a suit. Ladies would invite me in and I'm thinking they want cleaning fluids when all they really want is their pipes cleaned. G'Money's time don't come cheap and I made a lot of my sales that way. Almost all of the CMB was getting blessed daily like that. One customer even gave me a stack of money. The icing on the cake at this job was seeing the faces of those white boys week after week wondering how I pulled off more profits in the low end neighborhoods. Their reaction almost made up for the money I wished I was making...almost. Steady work was coming in and all but after food, rent and things you just need every month, there was nothing left really. A month had passed and I had regained most of my connects and tried to do it big but straight. Did a comedy show here and there and started throwing parties but it still wasn't enough. Finally I decided to try the welfare office again to see if I could at least get some food stamps to help with some of my expenses. I was at the welfare center and it just discouraged me again.

The day I went to the welfare center was the same day I received a call from my friend Ricardo. I thought maybe if I met up with him, maybe he'll give me $20 or something. He wanted me to meet him down at his Cousin Jose's club on 115th street. That night I was looking on point, you had to back then. The line was long and the club was jumping! It was like I was back in the Dominican Republic but New York style so it was bigger, smoother, and hotter. Girls were killing it on the dance floor. You know I had to grab two and show off. Ricardo and I were having fun and sometime during the night he leads me over to this table with these beautiful Latinas and Jose. This Latin brother looks serious like Tony Montana. He asks me to sit down and we start talking. Jose tells me he is a fan of my comedy show and the CMB Chunky Black. He lets me know that if I work for him he'd pull some strings to get Cedric out of jail sooner. Having someone know all about you and your close friends when you don't know them from Jack is a bit scary. Keeping my feelings to myself I just kept listening. If you listen carefully you will know everything that needs to be said, that why we got two ears and one mouth. Turns out Ricardo and his cousin Jose were sitting on two-three shopping bags filled to the top with coke. Since they knew I knew people out here in New York, they were willing to cut me in on a deal.

G'Money had tried the straight game but still couldn't find the rules where you win big only playing straight. It was frustrating that after so long my research still hadn't taught me how to make big money righteously. The potential money being offered was too tempting, I had too many bills, I missed my old lifestyle and everything about the deal checked out. He gave me 14 grams, and I gave it to 14 major hustlers in Harlem and that opened the door. I felt as if I hit the lottery. Just like that G'Money was back in the drug game. Mind you I never stopped the other things I was doing. Dewayne helped keep the cleaning stuff flowing for me, Stacey got me back into Chunky Black because that was his thing and Russell just did whatever whenever. You can never really tell what Russell is up to. As soon as all my connects found out G'Money was up and running again, the flood gates busted open. Business was great! I had people calling me every day. Then it started getting spooky. Lots of people were asking me to bring them a kilo. I wasn't bringing anybody a key so they could kill me and take the kilo! I wasn't having anybody do me like that. So I had them give me the money first and then I would give them the key. Best part about that was my custies that had that kind of paper always seemed to call with one or two more jobs attached to the order. Bookings came in for comedy shows, party promotion, cleaning supplies and travel engagements. I was doing shows in all the biggest spots from New York to Boston, Hollywood to Washington. At one point my Mastermind duplicated itself again and I started a production company representing various artists. This was to make sure I didn't miss out on any profits when someone asked me for entertainment on dates when G'Money was already taken. Life was getting back to normal again,

Baby you don't know what living is 'till you've lived it up in the 70's! "I'm talking Studio 54 Thursdays and Club Fever Fridays". Everybody was passing through New York and they all wanted me at their functions because I had the goods. Everyone was sniffing dope. I became friends with some of the top celebrities in show business. These people shared everything from their lovers to their check books. They all loved me and I loved their money.

Once Ricardo saw just how good I was doing for myself, he invited me over to his house one night and said, "Papi, let me tell you something just between you and me o.k.? Mira, you don't have to buy all this. Just buy 8 ounces. You cut it like this, with baking soda and you give them the kilo and you make $8000."

Shocked I said, "You mean to tell me that if I mix this with baking soda like you're doing on the table, it won't show that I did that?"

He said, "No, Gerald, no. One ounce makes two ounces; two ounces make four ounces; four makes eight; eight makes sixteen. Like this Papi"

I went and made $8000 on my first drop. This one guy I was dealing with was selling every two days; he was coming to me every two days. Two was my magic number. I was making a 50% profit on everything that I bought and sold. I was getting cash, money. I had so much money I was swimming in it like Scrooge McDuck. This new power I possessed made me drunk. Like an addict G'Money wanted more money because money seemed to buy me anything I wanted, nothing was off limits. My Mastermind had finally figured out how to duplicate to a level where it could let the business run itself while I ventured out to find new territory to conquer.

First, I sought out that girl Michelle from back in the day. Even though I knew a man was in her life, I didn't care. I trusted my money, my game and I wanted her back. She floated in and out of the clubs but I was usually too busy to give her the attention she needed and deserved. Found out she was still living at home in Esplanade Gardens so I went over there late one night. When I saw that shy smile peeking through the cracked open door, my heart melted. It took me a minute but eventually I convinced her to go up to the roof with me where I set up some champagne and candles. Michelle was a good girl so since she had a man we didn't do anything but drink and keep each other warm. I swear I saw her cheeks blush when I told her how long I've been wanting this. Her heart beat was so fast and strong but she still wouldn't kiss me. Things felt like the candlelight, view and my affections for her were a bit much and things were getting too hot not to go anywhere. I offered her money, cars, jewelry and time but she still wouldn't let me get some. Out of respect, I suggested I excuse myself but not before letting her know I was coming back for her in the near future.

She came in close and with a light flick of her tongue; Michelle kissed my neck softly behind the ear and quietly said, "I hope so." Then she went downstairs leaving me alone on the roof.

The image of her body walking away really got to me. I was going to have to somehow clean up my act while maintaining this lifestyle to be able to live with a girl like Michelle the way I wanted. A cool chill was taking over the city but I didn't feel it still remembering how warm Michelle's body was against mine. She left me open and when I looked inside I found what money could never get you. I thought about my parents living in the Dominican Republic and the beautiful fulfilling righteous life they lived. They looked at me, Gerald, their eldest son whom they gave everything to now running one of the biggest dope/ crack/ cocaine operations in the country. How would they think of me? Word out on the street said it was my guys that broke up families. We seduced their able bodied children into decadence with money and fifteen minutes of fame. Young, old, strangers, friends, family, everyone was fair game and viewed as a potential customer. Little Gerald had grown up to become a Drug Lord. No real love or respect would ever be given to someone with that title unless it was coming from some damn fools and what's the honor in that? Looking over New York City late at night I could see how I and Nino Brown got seduced by the game. They surrounded us from youth with these lights, glamour and power but it was all costume jewelry compared to the real thing. It could all be taken away just like that with the click of a gun. Nino Brown got caught and now I too foolishly made myself a target again.

In that moment up there, I craved the one thing my Father and Uncles had that I couldn't offer to anyone or myself and that was real security and deep rooted love. Suddenly, Stacey bust onto the roof and comes over to me saying, "You alright? I came up because you were standing so close to the edge of the ledge and it looked like there was a fire starting up. I see now it was just you doing your thing. Look, I got three girls in a limo downstairs. Why don't you bring the rest of that champagne and join us?"

I was in need of anything to get my mind off of this, because I wasn't ready for that journey yet; it was just too much for me to handle. The Mastermind had to be turned back onto our business and Stacey had the right medicine for my ailment. When I woke up the next night, I could feel I had changed. This grind on the streets and in the drug world had turned G'Money into a "cold hearted gangster". I was detached from love and since GOD is love it meant I had really cut myself off from my blessings and foolishly couldn't even see it.

Chapter 7

The Fall

You never know how far you can fall until you hit rock bottom. When Crack hit the streets, a lot of things changed. President Reagan was denouncing drugs with every "Don't Do Drugs" Commercial. He was talking about AIDS, guns and the Prison Industrial System. From every law that passed, every prison they built, every disease made is someone else's payday, someone else's hustle. Illegal drugs are this country's top business with employees and customers around the globe. A business gives its customers what they want. Heroin and Cocaine had never been purer or cheaper despite the massive investment into the war on drugs informing the nation that Crack was addictive and deadly. Whether you were a junky or a dealer, it was a good time to be in the game. Most times you end up being both.

That life had taken me over. Back then you weren't cool unless you were doing drugs, had three or more lovers and lots of money, talent or both. I had all four which made me high in demand. It was the late 70's early 80's. I had access to all of the happening spots. There wasn't a club or party I couldn't get into or wasn't profiting from. Everyone in New York knew who I was from the homeless junkies on the streets to the guys that just flew in on their private jets for a fun night in the city that never sleeps. Anyone and everyone you could think of was hitting up some kind of drug and the CMB was there to provide. G'Money was in honey! History shows us that whenever a black man puts his all into something he flips it, puts his spin on it and that thing transforms itself into the next fad. Where ever I was at, people knew they'd also find the next best thing on the market. My empire even helped put Hip Hop into the main stream through its entertainment division GM Productions. The CMB represented acts like Curtis Blow, Diana Ross, and Gladys Knight and the Pips. People still call me to this day thanking me for what I've done towards the advancement of Black culture in society. It was like I had the Midas touch, anything I put my hand in started blowing up like crazy! Next thing I know I turn around and even Hollywood is paying tribute to me and the CMB by putting out the movie "New Jack City™." I couldn't believe they had made a movie about me and Nino Brown!" They even knew about me saying, "Am I my brother's keeper? YES I AM!" The whole thing blew my mind. In the streets of Harlem and all the underground spots around the world, G'Money was crowned the latest Drug Lord Icon. This is something I'm not proud of. Because of God and God's love I am redeemed today.

There's something you should know about illegal substances and the world you become a part of when you get involved. It influences you to become ego driven. Vanity, sexuality and selfish aims become more important to you then family and life. The more you do, the cockier you get and as you go deeper you start getting sloppy and paranoid. All over Harlem I had look outs, cameras, escape routes, armed body guards, paid off police officers, stand by getaway cars with drivers, you name it I bought it because in my mind I knew someone powerful was after me. G'Money was wanted because even though I had money and gave money, I was also ruthless with people that owed me money and it didn't matter what their status was in society or where they lived. It was the drug lord game to me and I was living it out making threats, threatening violators, marking my territories by using violent bullies and sexing up all the beautiful women that crossed my path along the way.

One day, I got a surprise call by this Diana Ross looking woman from Staten Island that I had a couple of one night stands with. Shocked, I listened as she let me know I had fathered a child. Oh my GOD, Oh thank GOD for keeping me healthy all my life and giving me a handsome son that I love with everything I've got, even if I don't always show it. Hey, you know how men get sometimes, please forgive me.

When I first found out about my son, I did try to do the right thing. Since the CMB Empire was now running itself, I was able to move out to Staten Island and get me a nice little spot there to set up shop. My Diana Ross look alike had turned into the Fat Lady because of the pregnancy and I was very vain back then. Of course, I willingly gave her all the money she asked for but her yapping mouth coupled with the drugs I was on made me very impatient. After that relationship ended, I fell for this hot girl Messinda that I quickly moved into my spot with me. Now Messinda was nice looking and my girlfriend but no one could stop me from doing what I was doing especially not after Staten Island helped me discovered how in demand crack was. There was this woman that worked on Wall Street and lived upstairs from us. Messinda started getting jealous and very upset because I'd drop everything to make money off of a customer and this woman was buying coke and she would come back to me every twenty-five minutes for a gram of this coke. This one evening I went up there and she was half naked in some black lingerie asking me if I know how good my stuff was. I told the woman I had to go but she stopped me and asked for me to wait because she had something to show me and wanted to buy more. I maintained my cool with that so I sat down, looked and yo, she was cooking it up! She was doing what they called "freebasing". To some guys freebasing is better than sex, and some guys will tell you that. She said it gets her aroused and it would turn her on. Most people who are under the influence would do anything and I was weak and you know the flesh is weak, so I surrendered to the temptation. I was wrong. Very wrong to do that to my girlfriend.

She walked over to me and placed my hands over her body and said, "Don't leave me here alone again feeling this way all by myself." You know this was a lie, look at how that sounds and me and my dumb self I fell for all the lies. Think about it. She wasn't "my woman" talking about talking about don't leave me here alone. It wasn't my responsibility to leave her alone. If you ever have somebody tell you that line, "Don't leave me here alone again," RUN don't WALK out that door! But I fell for it and gave in to the temptation. When I think about it now, I know it was the influence of sex. There wasn't any love there. You know that love is special and intimate with someone you care for. But sex and romance, all of that combined with the influence of drugs can get you caught up in the trap of temptation. She influenced me; with her sexy strut, the lingerie and the drugs. I certainly did not make my best judgment on that day...

But now I'm looking at it from another perspective. I know now that I was going the wrong way. I hope people can learn from my experience and I hope she's clean now and wherever she is today she's no longer using drugs. I'm proud to say I know the difference now about the power of the influence. You have to be careful what you indulge in. If you're not, you could end up caught up.

They say, "A fool and his money shall soon part". Before I knew it...my pants were open, my mouth was on the pipe and that was the last nail in the coffin. I had the strongest stimulants in the world. Sex and drugs are the strongest influences in the world. It became a force of habit and it put me in a position where I was obsessed with getting high and having sex. Overnight, I was addicted to hitting the drugs hard-core and fell off of my grind so I started losing money fast. Right around that same time, phone calls were coming in from Russell, Stacey and Dewayne telling me some federal organizations above the cops was shutting down all of my establishments. Of course, the calls were also coming in from my baby's momma and Jose both looking for money. But because of the drugs my Mastermind could no longer stay calm and collected under all the pressure.

Ricardo came looking for me and when he found me it was obvious he felt bad about the position I had put myself in. I owed Jose around 20k, my empire he watched grow was falling apart and here I was coked out on the stuff he introduced me to. He sobered me up as best he could and let me know it was time to take a break from the game. I fought him on it at first because I didn't want him taking away my drugs and best source of money. Patiently, Ricardo helped my mind understand how stupid I sounded. Apparently, the New York State Government had a price on my head and both he and Jose were moving back to the Dominican Republic to get out of the heat. He suggested I do something the same. My argument at that point was obsolete and not worth pressing. Ricardo then asked me where Jose's money was. I told him truthfully what happened so Ricardo let me know he was going to pay off my debt as a gift for having helped in making his family super rich.

Do you understand how lucky I was being let off of the hook with what I owed? Jose was one of those drug dealers that were known for being crazy. Let me explain: The way it usually works is you get the drugs from one guy. For example, say you receive 30,000 worth on credit. That means you owe the guy who gave you the drugs 30,000 worth. This same guy, unbeknownst to you, sends out some people to break into your house. Sometimes it's a stealth professional locksmith. Sometimes a crew of men in masks to tie up your entire family. They steal the drugs from you and now this guy has his 30,000 worth that he originally gave you but now you also owe him double the original amount: 60,000 stacks. But, it was easy to get rid of the guy you owe the money to. So I guess that's what probably bought the homicide rate up across the country during the early 90's. Can you imagine having to deal with that? Because I was at the top of my game, I didn't have to deal with those types of people much. So at the time, I never knew the game was so hard until later on in life when you hear stories from people who were deep in the game like that.

Sober and realizing how many days I had spent away from Messinda, Ricardo dropped me off at my place in Staten Island before saying his good byes. She was so upset. Everything came out and then silence. Over the next few days, the shakes got me real bad but I got well very fast. We got word that Jose was shot and killed the day before he was supposed to get on his flight out of here. Everything around me was falling apart but a lot of people couldn't see because the CMB Empire still had a heartbeat. Messinda heard the news about Jose and freaked wondering if I was next. A few phone calls later we were packed up and on our way to her brother's house in Boston. Using up the rest of the money we had on the move seemed worth it considering what might happen if we stayed in New York. Messinda also thought that maybe taking me out of New York would help cure my addictions. G'Money was moving to Springfield Boston to retire from the drug game. When we got to her brother's house, after he helped us unpack he kicked me out and threw me on a bus back to the city! Messinda's brother humiliated me and I was too broken down to defend myself. All he left me with was one bag of clothes.

The whole ride back sobered me up real good. How dare he treat G'Money like that! That ungrateful, betraying Messinda let him do it too. Damn shame. If they had done this to me three months earlier I would have beat him down to a pulp. My problem was that I was asleep for so long that now I had no money and I had detached myself from all my connects trying to clean up for that hoe. There was no way I was going to let them get away with that. It was time to rise up again for a third time. Step one was finding a job so I could have some money in my pocket. The bus pulled into the Port Authority. I found a place to leave my bag and grabbed an abandoned used newspaper to check out the wanted ads. GOD must have liked that I was trying to do things legit again because I found a traveling sales job that same day. What's better? It was for a cleaning products company. Ironically, a bus was leaving that day to their training site out in New Jersey and it was paid training!

The way they ran this company was superb. Top of the line. There were tons of training materials, classes and on-site training with real customers. I was one of like 70 people. Check out this scam from the company I worked for.

Once you got to the hotel where they held all of their seminars they tell you, yes you are getting paid but some of that money is being used to pay for your hotel and the rest they would hold to cover your supplies when it's time to go out into the field. When you finally do start training on the field, they drive you to and from the sites so you don't have to pay transportation but you do have to pay for the hotel and the supplies. Moving up their pyramid gave you a greater percentage of the profits from your sales but that took so long. A bunch of the people at the place told me they felt they had been kidnapped and being held prisoners. No one ever was allowed to make enough money to leave if you wanted to and there was this bonus you were entitled to being held over your head like a carrot. When were you supposed to receive the bonus? No one knew but it was big and you already worked for it so a lot of the people decided that after all the time they put in, there was no way they'd leave without that money. Now G'Money was here because it was free room and board while I picked myself back up. These other people, 90% of them were willingly being duped. You know me. I started taking notes on how they ran things because this company was money hand over foot thanks to their business model. The Mastermind's wheels starting spinning, in no time I had a plan I didn't have enough money to leave but I had enough to copy all of their materials little by little, day by day. When I had enough stuff to replicate their business, I used the little allowance they gave me to call some people and I broke out of that joint!

My peeps were real happy to see me. After filling the CMB in on what happened, I got down to business. First, I had my entertainment company book me a few shows up in Boston. If Messinda and her brother thought they had seen the last of me, they were about to have a rude awakening. Second, I had my team make our own fliers, pamphlets and training materials using what I got from that cleaning products company as a template. The guys were amazed at how I reshaped the cleaning products division of the CMB Empire to resemble the other company in places where my business model needed obvious improvement. I had learned my lessons well and now I was ready. Wait till you hear what I did next! That cleaning products company owed me money and tried to play G'Money remember? Well, after I reorganized my cleaning products business, I got back on the bus and went back up there. In undercover mode, I offered all my fellow classmates that I left behind, a chance to do the same thing at a bigger percentage cut for them in money making Manhattan. Ha ha! I ended up taking 80% of their employees away! Remember what I said earlier, you keep learning from those that have been successful and adjust yourself until you find what works for you. Winners always stay in the game one way or another because winning is the goal.

For my next move, I went to perform a few shows up in Boston. Now Boston at that time was a good place for business connections. After hanging out in their night clubs, I was an overnight sensation! Ask people that know me, they know how good I am at my craft. Boston was sold and I made sure my name was everywhere so that my ex would know I was back on top and she was having no part in it. Boston's entire high end rich crowd loved having me around. They wanted to have me up there like every weekend. You know how these elite folks are; hanging with them in the club night after night I started developing my drinking habit on the down low. Some people might say alcohol isn't a drug because it's legal but I'm here to tell you it is. Alcohol has the power to open you up to things you wouldn't normally see or feel. Some of that stuff is spiritual and not always positive. Ask folks that drink; they know what I'm talking about. The more I hung around those people from Boston and their ways, I started noticing their drug habits and the potential to make over 50% profit just like when I was working with Jose. I thought about how things were before Messinda convinced me to pause on my game. Desperation to get back into the position where my status was on top overtook me and temptation won. See I wasn't thinking right because after I made the adjustments to my cleaning company, it was now starting to make the big bucks I had hoped it would originally. I didn't really need this extra business but I was seduced again by the limelight with a splash of revenge from what Messinda's brother did to me. Plus I told you what drugs can do, they make you think and rationalize things funny.

Not to toot my own horn, but G'Money is smart and I was looking to get the most profits out of this town. My Mastermind observed the territory, set up pawns and went to work. All I know is I was visiting there a lot but I never used my money to get things, never rented a hotel room and sure in hell never looked to buy a spot.

Actually G'Money had the harem set up for real. Check this out man, while I was out there I mostly was staying at a whorehouse called Mama Anala's! Now Mama Anala was this attractive black woman with two white Indian ponytails! And Mama Anala could smoke and drink you under the table! She would smoke up almost an ounce and you know what she'd tell you? She'd say, "That wasn't shit!" She liked me so much she made it so that I was the only man allowed to sleep over there. All of these girls were coming in from Detroit and Chicago and this is where they stayed to wait for their pimps to take them out wherever they were going to work at. It was like a layover house. A whole book could be written on the stories I could tell you about this place man. If the walls could talk, they'd tell you about all of the graphic details and you'd be left with your mouth wide open! :O

75

Comedy was good and I had my feelers out ready to collect some money whenever the opportunity presented itself. All while I was dealing drugs up there I never used them and I never got into any real trouble. Then I met a self-made millionaire, whose name was Ms. Lucky. Her boyfriend was a football player with the Giants. When I met her, that relationship was ending. She was an older woman, but she looked young. She had a mustang convertible, a Mercedes convertible and she had a Jaguar. Ms. Lucky gave me access to her club and her clothing store.

Ms. Lucky also knew that I was involved with promoting parties in New York and she had a joint called the "The Boom Boom Room" (changed the name to protect the innocent). There was also a bar and restaurant in the Ballroom. I used to go in there and get me some milk, some chopped ice, some Kahlua and some rum. That's when I started drinking heavily and that's when I started carrying a gun because I always had a lot of money on me. The cops never bothered me because they always came into the Ballroom to eat but that alcohol had me paranoid.

Eventually Ms. Lucky convinced me to move up there with her and that lasted for a long time. At one point, Ms. Lucky was out of town and had me handling some business for her where she gave me $4000 dollars to make a deposit. Some guy convinced me to go to New York and buy some drugs. I flipped her $4000 dollars and made $8000 dollars with it. I would double my money every couple of days. So, I'm bringing the coke back and I'm dibbling and dabbling in it and I started getting high with the coke. Ms. Lucky also started getting high. But the thing about Ms. Lucky was that she had a strong tolerance. Her tolerance was so strong you couldn't even tell she was high unless I told you. But me, I was feeling it and it made me paranoid just like the alcohol did. So both Ms. Lucky and I got into a lot of altercations. At one point, I took my pistol and waived it in the air! I was just going crazy with the drugs and everything. I had such a long run and then all of a sudden, I was irrational. I was just out of my mind when it came down to using drugs. To make a long story short, I knew it was time to leave. When I moved out of Ms. Lucky's house, I needed a U-Haul truck just for my clothes! And then I went from riches to rags. Oh Brother!

When you're hitting hard drugs and you get clean but then get back on it again, most of the time the addiction comes back worse than before. Ms. Lucky made me bring all my stuff back to New York. It was gone in no time because I was drugged out. Nothing mattered to me. Not my empire, not my friends, NOTHING! I didn't want to have any responsibilities. I didn't want to pay any bills. I started thinking outlandish thoughts. It finally dawned on me that when you're not homeless you have to pay all these bills. You have to pay rent, you had to buy clothes, shop for food and you had to get haircuts and all that stuff. I didn't care about any of that. I had four or five places where I could stay. That's when I decided I wanted to be homeless. Deciding to be homeless was reckless but my mind was coked out and being homeless was a choice. At that point, it seemed as if I had nothing to lose. When you have nothing to lose, you just don't care about anything. I had family and relatives that I could have stayed with; aunts and uncles. But when you're out there drugging', you make that decision to hang out all night and do what you want to do, which is the wrong choice.

The places I stayed were like little rent-a-room centers. I would pay the person $20 or so dollars, get some sleep, and take a shower. A person could be okay with living like this as long as they had the money, which wasn't much; and I wasn't sleeping in every night. I was out doing what I wanted to do. It was a vicious cycle to be wrapped up in. As soon as you get a little money you always go back to the drugs and the life. You find someone, and say "I'm coming to spend the night". Then go get some groceries: some pancake mix, some ground beef, and some onions. I got about an eight ball too. But once the coke is gone, they're like, "'you gotta go!" If I had a little extra money on me they'd calm down, if I didn't have any money, they would kick me out. And I always felt like, damn, I've been kicked out of places better than this. The drug had such a hold on me; it caused me to stay out there and be homeless and accept that sort of punishment from people who only wanted me around when I had money.

This isn't a reason for a person to be homeless because they have facilities and programs to help get people off of the streets. You're only homeless because you want to be homeless and I didn't care to want to know any better. I never went to a shelter. I never went into the system to learn about all of these places where I could go and get help. I used to ride the train from 241st street to Far Rockaway and back and you have people waking you up on the train telling you about a shelter you can go to. I used to get up off the train and leave when I saw them talking to the other homeless people. I didn't want to hear any of that crap. As a homeless person, you have no protection; you don't even have an umbrella! I remember one night I got myself wet and forgot I had nowhere to go home to. My socks were so soaking wet and I didn't even care; I had to walk a mile to get high. The hardest part about being homeless is when you have to go to the bathroom real bad. There are places that you have to go in, like McDonald's and Burger King. I remember my socks were so stink. When I tried to take them off, they stuck to the bottom of my feet! The smell was so strong it was like putting ammonia to your face, it made you go, "WHEW!" I hopped the train at 135th street and I had just bought a pair of new socks. I went to the back of the car because I knew it would be empty and I took off my shoes, put on the clean socks that I just got, and threw the old socks in the train. I knew those socks stunk so badly because that train stayed empty. Everybody that got on that car said, "Ew! Oh God!" And they ran to the next car!

One day a brother came up to me and said, "Hey man, you want a sandwich?"

I said, "Yes, man, yes."

He gave me a banana and then asked, "You tired of living like this?"

In that moment of clarity I was broke and feeling sorry for myself so I opened up to him saying, "Yeah! I don't even want to tell you what it's like."

The guy comes back with, "That don't even matter. Do you believe in Jesus? You want to come with me?"

This was the early 90's and the streets were filled with freaks. I was messed up but I wasn't to the point where I would sell myself. I said, "Man, you ain't no gay are you? I don't play that man."

He laughed saying, "Nah brother. Do you want to come with me?"

What was this guy getting at? I asked him where and he told me he had a place where I could stay for free just a couple of stops away on the train. It was music to my ears because I had no idea what I was going to do before that man came up to me. I told the guy, "Ain't that a coincidence. Man, I swear... I'm going to take a chance with you bro because I'm real tired man."

This brother took me to a church. When I came in there these brothers gave me shirts, clean clothes... Christian brothers. Man, they loved me and they hugged me like I was a long lost relative. They took off my shoes. They gave me a pair of slippers. They gave me a new pair of underwear, a pair of socks, new pants. They washed my clothes. They gave me new clothes and a place to sleep. I woke up in the morning and went downstairs. They had women living there. They had guys there. We were all going to church in the afternoon; in the middle of the day. They were all about the word of God. I stayed there for two weeks. They tried to get me to do some work for them. They wanted me to

78

go to the welfare center and sign some papers where they would get the money that you got from the welfare office. Even if the welfare office didn't give them the money, they still got your money. They had a system where you paid for your stay. They fed me; got me fat. But they were also like I couldn't leave the premise for the first two weeks or something crazy like that; like they were monitoring me. I felt like I was in prison or something, so I was like, I have to get up out of here. I thought I had it all together.

I came out of that place and I must have been clean for two weeks. Then I bumped into Michelle and I thought, "Oh my GOD, today is my lucky day!" We started talking and walking and somehow we ended up in front of my man's crib. We stopped for a minute and then she enticed me to do something for her.

She said to me, "Listen, can you do me a favor and go upstairs and get one from Louie and them?"

Louie was my man and all that and I could go to Louie because they probably wouldn't serve her. But I told her, "Nah, I don't do that no more."

Michelle kissed me on my neck and said, "Come on baby, do this for me. I'll look out for you. You know".

I was sprung! Yeah this was all too familiar to me and I knew just what to ask for, "Look out for me how? Ooooooh shoot, are we talking Fellatio?"

Michelle looked me in the eyes and said, "Mm hm. Fellatio baby."

The minute she said that, I was ready to sprint so I said, "Okay. Hold on a second and I'll be right back." I went upstairs and I get the drugs for her. We went back to my little $20 a night spot. She comes in the room, drops her mink coat on the floor, slips off her skirt, and pulls down her panties. She's butt naked before I could even close the door and lock it. I'm looking at her and thinking how I ain't had none in a little while.

Michelle walks over to me saying, "Honey, you know what I do? You don't mind, do you?"

I grabbed her and whispered in her ear, "Yeah, I know what you do and nah, I don't mind."

That's when she pushed me between a rock and a hard place saying, "Do you want to get busy first?"

I could tell she was going to be a problem if I didn't do it with her. A lot of nice girls that got turned out were like that especially if they know you never seen them being bad. Before I knew it, I was doing my thing.

All of a sudden, Michelle said "Hold on a second man!"

I was sitting watching her from the floor and all of a sudden she took this stem out of her purse, set everything up and she took a hit. She motioned for me to come closer to her and then she exhaled

I put my pants back on, and said, "I'll be right back." Then I went down the block to my man and said, "Yo, let me get ten."

My friends were happy for me being clean so when I rolled up on him he said, "Man, what you talking' about?"

I needed to get back to Michelle. Frustrated I yelled, "I said give me ten!"

My friends wanted me back in the game and they knew I had to get clean to do that. Upset, he looked at me and said, "G, don't tell me you smoking' again?"

My eyes couldn't look him straight in the face. I knew they cared but I didn't. I pushed him and said firmly, "Don't worry about that, man. Just give me ten."

Just like that I was back off in the race. Unfortunately you can't get someone off of that treadmill until they want to and all I wanted right now was some drugs and Michelle. She started me up and that escapade wasn't just one night. We didn't leave the room for days. I was crazed with the drugs. You know what they say, one is too many and a thousand ain't enough.

Chapter 8

Organized Planning

You know what they say. If your first plan fails man...try another! I cannot express enough about the art of persistence! This is where the majority of men and women meet failure. You need to apply one plan after another until you achieve your goals.

Remember to build "sound" and "workable" plans each time. You also need to understand that when your plans fail, that the temporary defeat is not "permanent" failure. Don't quit because you've failed in your own mind. Many men and woman of American History finally acquired wealth because of their burning "desire" to be successful. If you think you "can" or you think you "can't"....your right! You have to change your way of thinking to be a powerful and respected Mastermind. Your leadership qualities determine your future. You must be organized and have the cooperation of others in order to carry out your plans effectively.

In order to move forward, you must have the courage to carry out decision making no matter how hard it is. Sometimes, it's assuming many risks. An example of such courage in American History would be the unwavering courage it took for 56 men to sign the "Declaration of Independence" in Philadelphia on July 4, 1776. Each and every one of them were so bold to make this momentous decision that would have cost them their lives. They also risked the lives of their family and their future as they changed history and gained "freedom" as they fought for a new civilization.

Not that every decision you make as a leader and Mastermind will be life or death, but this shows you a more dramatic look at how history was changed because of the cooperation of others.

You have to find your own people to be included in your Mastermind group. It can be as few or as many as you need to carry out your plan. Get as many people with specialized knowledge (people who know the genre of which you need to carry out your plan) as you can. If it's "Real Estate" then acquire people from that sector. If it's finance, then go after your best brokers etc.

Whatever it is, make sure your people are also qualified to perform the job. Do your diligence and make sure you don't ask someone to perform a task that you won't be ready to do yourself. Be fair and Just within the group. If done right, your group will follow you anywhere at any time. Make sure also to go over your plans often to make sure it makes sense to you and your team and that it is the most feasible plan you can carry out.

Figure out in those plans of yours just "how" you will compensate and benefit the group moving forward. Maintain group meetings as much as possible as you reenact your plans with the group and concentrate on the methods you will use to inevitably get everyone paid in the end.

Yeah Baby! Nobody is really born a leader! At one point you were a follower who listened intently to your Boss, Leader or Mastermind. Those who took down notes and took risks became their own Mastermind.

Ask yourself this man. What qualities of leadership do you possess? Write down your list man of the best attributes you possess as a qualified leader. You must have the utmost self-confidence and courage to make split second decisions for your group to succeed.

One of the most important factors in the mix of being a powerful leader is to keep a high level of respect. That's something that I know a lot about. Each and every one of my Mastermind group respected me because I kept a pleasing personality and was understanding to their strife whether it was inside the group or personal. I offered them my direction and experience to correct them before they went down the wrong path and had to endure hardship. I was able to stop them before it was too late.

Another quality that is a "must have" is to be fully organized. You must be ready to delegate corrected plans to your "lieutenants" so they can pass it down throughout your group correctly.

Here's another tip Baby! Don't be selfish and claim that all the success and Glory was because of your great Mastermind plan. Give people credit where credit is due. Nobody likes or will stay with a Cocky or arrogant leader. It just ain't gonna happen that way man. Create peace and harmony within the group and with you. Lead by encouragement and not by dictatorship. Listen to your group's questions and concerns. It will only enhance your strategy and competency as their leader.

In addition to knowing all your strengths within your group, you must also know their weaknesses. Either get rid of the weaknesses or use them to your advantage. Ask yourself pertinent questions like:

A/ Have I based my decisions on guesswork or true analysis and detailed thought?

B/ Have I reached my goal which I established?

C/ How can I improve my strengths and my personality for the greater good of the team?

D/ Have I maintained my persistence in pursuance of the team goal?

E/ What changes need to be made to be a better leader or have a better group?

F/ Procrastination cannot be tolerated! Do what you say!

G/ Is each team player you have in the right position for the job you gave him or her? If not, make some changes man. Remember, it's for the good of the whole team.

H/ Have you maintained a burning desire to succeed? Do you have the creative imagination it takes to move your plan forward to success?

I/ Are you influenced by autosuggestions to yourself by yourself? Be careful what you tell yourself. Keep walking a straight line and don't deviate from fame and fortune back to poverty level! You ARE what you think. Think "powerful" and you will be just that!

J/ Don't let anyone stand in your way! Surround yourself with supportive people whether it's your spouse, family or friends! That will help "boost" your Mastermind plan into desirable results man!

K/ Last but not least! Have "Faith" baby! See yourself that you have "already" assimilated great fortune or fame! Conduct yourself in such matters accordingly. Walk with confidence! And you will see the end results quicker and easier without the cloud of doubtfulness hanging over your head!

As I end this chapter, I want to tell each and every one of you that if you perceive, you will believe and you will achieve your goals! Any plan can be attainable if you keep moving forward with action, determination and faith that keep your positive emotions alive! Know deep down in your mind that your plan will work alongside the cooperation of others and your willingness to be open minded and the Law of Attraction will magnetize and attract the things, people and places needed to complete your journey and materialize your plans into fruition. Your endeavors must be built with truth and justice in mind or therefore it will never sustain longevity.

Set aside 30 minutes a day where you can be alone with your thoughts and see yourself already in your new home or new car! Thoughts become things so dream away people! Envision yourself in your new office with the hustle and bustle of a prosperous business that you created! FEEL yourself sitting in your new leather chair man with your prominent boss's desk! Look out your window to see the buzz and commotion outside! Walk into your boardroom to see your team sitting in their chairs waiting for your next command!

It doesn't matter where you live or at what level monetarily you are at now. It will all change when you change your mindset and develop and grow a plan of action that you cultivate and nurture to receive your end result. Keep doubt and indecision at bay! Keep your mind strong with conscious thoughts of positive mind control and don't listen to negative mind sets who tell you your dreams are not attainable! If that was the case, then we would never have had cell phones, cars, planes, computers, electrical appliances, TV's and the like! Those innovative inventors had to block out what the naysayers were saying; that it was impossible to achieve their goals.

I hope I inspired you to get your dreams moving into action! I wish you all much success. See you at the "Top" baby!!

Chapter 9

Resurrection: The Rebirth for Redemption

Step one used to be getting a job to put some money in my pockets but I knew then there was a step before that. I closed my eyes and got really still within myself. One by one I counted all of my blessings and felt the gratitude that God gave me. There is always someone that is worse off than you are; the key is pointing out to yourself what has gone right. For me, I was healthy, my parents were still alive, I had family, and I had experienced true friendship in life. My body was able and all my limbs were intact, the drugs didn't mess up my looks that much. My mind was still with me and after what I went through I could have gone crazy. My sense of humor was still intact. I could still smile and I had begun on my journey to truly know GOD. How often do you go over the things you have to be grateful for? There is always something, man I can point out to you at least two. One, you have life or you wouldn't be reading this book.

That means there is a chance for you to start again on something which is your number two. After thinking about all that stuff, it's time for part II of the exercise which is to confront your fears. There are a lot of guys that get out of jail on the right path then get caught up again when they get back home and find themselves back behind bars before they can even truly realize they were out and free. There was no guarantee that I wasn't going to end up like one of those guys and that's what scared me most. I really wanted to do things right this time. Taking the time out to look at what my weaknesses might be helped me to better guard myself when temptation reared its ugly head. Now step one is something that needs to be done every day no matter how good things get.

Step two was getting a job. Going out into the streets or reaching out to my connects after spending a stint in jail for a few months on a B.S. charge was not an option. So I dropped my stuff off at my cousin's again, got the paper and found a job. Playing it safe felt like the right thing to start with but sometimes you have one way and GOD has another idea. I got fired from that job at a local store chain. I felt that was a blessing for me to move forward again. It was time for me to reconnect with my friends and catch up on what had been missed. I gathered all of the CMB together, Stacey, Russell, Dewayne and Cedric. Turns out, we still had GM Productions, The cleaning service and New York's Own Hollywood.

My life is here for others to learn from as I ascend up towards that 1%. Every day, I still run into people on the same paths that have gotten wealthy legitimately. Step number one, which was my last addition to my formula for success, seems to be the one major common link we all have. Strength, knowledge and great wisdom come out of the stillness. The Mastermind has also continued to duplicate itself to now include CMS also known as Cash Money Sisters. Since you have traveled with me this far I think it's time that I introduced you to the team and what they're about today. We held a red carpet event and the powers that be tried to stop it! They were certain that if the CMB was back together with former Drug Lord Icon G'Money that there must be drugs involved. But my history has taught me it's best to go legit or quit. We as an empire have new aims now. What's our goal? I'll tell you; our goal is to better humanity by helping more good men and women into that 1%. Good things are the ones that last while the rest burns away with time. I'm still performing and I'm still wanted. So many people can't seem to figure out how men and women can generate wealth without the help of the special interest but I am an example of how you can. Feel free to study me, learn from my mishaps and avoid my mistakes.

Trust me it wasn't easy to get to where I am today. I had a lot of rough mountains to climb. I remain persistent! I was left all worn and torn up after being bruised from the battlefield, but the falls did not discourage me. I kept getting back up and I kept the mentally that I would never give up, because giving up will get you nowhere in life. No matter how tough times got for me, I knew that soon it would be over and there was something prosperous out there awaiting me.

All of my troubles and woes seemed inescapable. It seemed like there was no way out. But then I found a way out. And the way out was finding God. The beginning of my redemption was a transition into a rude awakening. As I experienced my change of newness, I had to change my mind set and the way that I viewed everything. You see, what I learned through my experiences is that you must keep your mind first of all because everything is a battle of the mind.

It is a battlefield of the mind every day that we live. What we hold in our thoughts, what we hear from spoken words, what is televised that has a visual effect, and what is printed in the news affects us mentally. These images linger in our heads...when we see stories of real life murders and terror going on in the world that we live in. If you take the fear out of terrorism there would be no terror. Terror is when you don't have a sound mind. When you're afraid to live and face another day because you feel like the next day might be your last. But when you have God, you don't have to live in fear.

When drama, trials and tribulations and destruction come at you, no weapon formed against you shall prosper. You have the power to bring destruction to its knees. All that you have to do is stand on a confirmation of what the Commander in Chief says about it. Then you will know his righteousness and then you will apply that righteousness. Then you can stand firm and strongly believe that there is no fear here in your realm. You have to make it precise. There is no fear here, and you have to repeat those words a couple of times so that you can gain the confidence that there is no fear or worries within you.

What I disclose to you is what I believe. That in itself has helped to conclude my thoughts on what it is to have a sound mind. In order to have peace within your soul, you need a sound mind and you need to be free from fears, worries and stress. A sound mind is oneness with God. When you have a sound mind you have Godly wisdom. See, God wants you to obtain his words and keep his saying at God's will for man. His will is to have God's words upon our lips all the days of our lives. We need to keep his words and instructions, to watch carefully and listen closely to the directions he has given to us.

But man has chosen to follow his own way and speak of things he has heard of throughout traditions and denominations. Men have used their own ways of thinking to misconstrue the truth. But a lie can never be the truth and the truth can never be a lie.

Theologically, man has learned how to take the word and apply it to his way of thinking. But when you have a sound mind, your words are lined up with God and not with your own way of thinking. When your words are lined up with God, you have the skillful Godly wisdom, and will not think in a worldly way. Wisdom is free to all and will come to those who seek her. For those who come to God for wisdom it will be received. You just have to ask unto him that is God who has all authority to make things come to pass. God is not a man that he shall lie, but as a seeker of the truth. God said "When a man knows wisdom, he knows the word of God." God is the only truth. I will pour out my spirit and make my words known to you. Well, I leave that with you for you to examine the truth that I have spoken. We're talking about redemption and in truth redemption is the only way out.

Redemption is taking what was old and making it new. That's why we have to get rid of the old mind set and approach things with a new mind set. We have to surrender in order to receive. Some things we have to sacrifice. You have got to give up what the relatives are saying about things and what mamma and them and all of our immediate people who are still experiencing the trials and tribulations on a day to day basis are saying.

You have to give up all of the talk of sickness, poverty, disease, ill health and lack. God is not into lack; he is into the abundant life. God said I set aside a good life, an abundant life for those who love me. And with the abundant life, there is nothing missing, nothing broken and nothing needed. There is nothing wanted, but in the kingdom of God it doesn't lack. So you have to be careful how you think. I share that with you because I want you to be aware of how to renew the structure of your life and the things around you. You can use a form of meditation and as you meditate it can only bring a positive mind set into the atmosphere and remove all of the negativity.

At the same token, be careful what you are hearing, for the measure of thought and study will be measured back on to you. These are the things we have to examine but pondering on the word and the things we need to know I think is so important. What it is we need to stand on matters the most. What I love about God is that he keeps you from the evil women. From the flattery of the tongue and from the seductions of a loose woman. Lust not after her beauty in your heart. See, you have to know that what's behind the word has been told for a purpose and seek the truth behind it. Anyone can look at a word and not perceive what is in a word. You have to stay there and analyze it in order to see the truth. You have to stay there and meditate on it and ponder on it until you have a better understanding. It has to become real and then it gives you more meaning of that which was read.

I've never taught in an education system. I mean I'm no professor, but I confess the truth that I have learned. Maybe I would have been a teacher and would have obtained a master's degree. But this world would not allow me to teach in that area. However, then there are some things they have learned through the system of operation in the kingdom of God. They have no acknowledgement of how to operate under the influences of God. If they operate by God's word they can live the abundant life. But I say all that to speak about pondering on the word of God. Some things will become real. Sometimes God will bring you back an experience. God will bring you an answer and you will know for a fact there's no way you could have gotten that answer which you received without the wisdom of God.

I remember reading the Bible one night about a story that was told about how you don't "have" to remember. They will help you to remember, remind and teach you the things which I have told you. When Jesus said, "I have to go out to prepare a way and I'm going to send you another helper. I'm going to send you the Holy Spirit, which will come back to teach you, tell you, and remind you." He gave exact details to guide us and told us clearly... But first of all, Jesus said "You have to take my word and stay there with it. You know my word is life. I didn't come here to condemn you, so anything that is going on in this world that's condemning is this world's way."

He demonstrated to us by telling us and showing us through examples of how to conduct ourselves and his teachings through miracle works and the journey he took us on and the price he paid for us to save us.

But he made this world for you to understand that I can give you my thoughts and my word. I need to be able to make my words known to you. I need you to meditate day and night. Jesus didn't say meditate just for today or at Sunday school or in church and all of these things are going to come to pass. He said meditate day and night. That means find a scripture and hold on to it, take that scripture and plant it in your heart like a seed and guard it. The evil one comes to snatch away what was sowed in your heart, for the things that will go on in the world that will bring about destruction and things that will turn you away from the word of truth and make you walk out of the love of God. But you have to remain in the love of God. Real genuine love with God and the wisdom of God's love is to love one another. Well the purpose of why God gave us love was to show how much we love him with all our hearts, our minds, our souls and our strength.

Don't be yoked to a poverty mentality. Some people will say that it's not nice to talk about people who don't have and that are lacking and that are poverty stricken. But that is a sustaining law and that law has been set into operation for those who aren't operating in the right law. In doing so that will cancel that law, because the kingdom of God is higher than this earth and standing so much greater. God says "My thoughts are not your thoughts; my ways are not your ways". God said that to the whole world man!

God doesn't have to answer to the world; the world has to answer to God. As a gangster, I was taught never to fear any man. I was able to enter into a place and I felt the confidence that I wasn't afraid of twenty-five or thirty men in a room. When my presence walked in, what I fear most disappeared!! And when I walked in, I was greeted with great respect. Which if I had kept my imagination that bad things were gonna happen, like if I would be destroyed by these men, then that could tear me up inside and I wouldn't be able to conduct myself because of being afraid and timid. But that wasn't the case because I walked with confidence and leadership!

I would never be able to handle the situation and come out as a victorious winner if I was scared out my mind, and that's the key. The power is the ability to get results. And it's so much I can embark upon, but that in itself can demonstrate to you what to practice. What you can receive let it be guarded in your heart, as a seed down deep to the root. That root is your relationship that God is the gardener and Jesus is the vine and we are the branches that comes out of the vine. God breaks off branches that don't stay in the vine. Man, man, man...that's the good stuff, but the hardship, man knows better. Paul said, "When I keep my mind on the word of God, it produces Godly thinking." That means my thoughts are pure, loving, kind and gentle. Who could hold you and blame you for everything if you conduct yourself in love? Do not step out of the circle and get angry, do not step out of the circle and go with other doers that are doing evil. Separate yourself from this.

Paul said, "My words produce my thoughts" and you know they are worldly emotions. God gave us emotions and he never intended for emotions to govern our lives. He wanted us to take charge over our emotions, so we are not moved by what we see. We are not moved by what we hear, we are only moved by what the word and God has to say. When you get to that level and that position man it's something that you know you have the power and you are planted like the rock of Mt. Zion. Unable to be removed and able to abide forever, that's how you have to learn to hold firm your acknowledgement of the word and stay there. It's not like just tonight we're just talking about it. We are just expanding our time to construct our soul that is being replenished by the promises that have been promised to those who will love him. So learning how to have those emotions and control your emotions is the key. You've got to do better to show God you've mastered your emotions. You're NOT supposed to get angry and mad to show people how crazy you can be or how bad and bitter you are. That's not the purpose in having the emotions to govern your life and to govern your emotions. Paul said "My words produce my thoughts, my thoughts produce my emotions, my emotions produce my decisions, my decisions produce my actions, my actions produce my habits, my habits produce my character and the destination where I will end up." I'll give you another example; Paul said "when I keep my mind on the word of God, it produces Godly thoughts, Godly emotions that I realize why God gave me emotions. He gave me emotions so I could have compassion to be able to love one another. In other words, I've been on this earth all of this time. I was supposed to walk in love every challenge and everything that I've been involved in."

I also was supposed to walk in love. I was supposed to remain in love. There are times where there are things that will get you to walk out of love. But be strong and stay in that circle because when you step out of that circle you're subject to sickness, disease, poverty, ill-health and lack.

I do not want to step out of that circle. I only bring these things to the attention of the reader and to the listener that you may receive the living word of God bringing forth greatness and the force of operating in the family of God. I hope this has enlightened you in sharing my Auto Biography with you of Redemption. When fear is there love is absent and when love is there fear is absent. So we have to learn always, always stay in love. No matter what. You will be tested!

I remember one time there was this incident where there were many people yelling and screaming just because I waited after what could have turned into a situation. If it wasn't for the fact that I was redeemed it could have escalated so I remained patient. My response was real humble and I told them forget about all the strife and bitterness. Maybe you and I can resolve this and I walked away with knowing I had results of accomplishing the power of love. I recognized the depth of what they were experiencing and that was strife, bitterness and resentment they had toward other people. A girl told me there that she appreciated how I handled this situation. She couldn't believe that a black guy like me could be so calm. Then somebody came running out of the office! This lady came back with nine guys and three security guards to find out who was looking for her. Then, when she heard it was me looking for her and heard how cool, calm and collective and kind I was she decided to let the goons go! She saw I could handle myself in a crisis. If I had been a real old gangster with my old mind-set I probably would have snatched her up and told them I got her. Because of the renewal of my mind, I was grateful that the girl came out and spoke to me so I could show them that you never judge a man by the color of his skin, but by the character of the man. But, God had put a new character in me and the new character that he put in me allowed me to be nice and to walk out of that office with ten-thousand dollars!

I've been in other similar situations and it was not just about the money. When I walked out of that office with ten-thousand dollars, I realized that I did not want to go back to my old life style. That would be like the old gangsters that will put you in a trunk and take you for a ride, and handcuff you to a tree in the woods. No one can hear you scream and the bugs and flies would eat you up alive. When you come back you would be deranged because of the mosquitoes and the bites that happen to you. Now you wouldn't want that to happen again so you would leave the area so you couldn't be found!

How can a man change his ways unless he changes the way he thinks? He has to learn how to love, show kindness and be gentle. With practice, you will learn how to achieve the greatest reward in life that you can imagine. When the praises go up, the blessings come down. In other words, the heavens are hearing those who have good faith and confidence in the love of God.

Paul, Timothy, John, Matthew, Isaiah, and Joseph are all impacted between the oneness in the change that they are connected with. Now we all have the power to remove the burdens and destroy the yokes and strong holds. One thing I can say for sure is if you ask you shall receive and if you seek you shall find, and knock and the door will open. So I say that to you to give you the hope and the confidence that you have in the world today and that you have took the time to hear a story of a servant that once was a gangster, and to show you God said that he is going to get rid of the hustlers, the pimps, the prostitutes and the murderers and I'm going to bring them back and I'm going to put them on shelves as new creatures that walks in the things of God. And I want you to know there is an opportunity for you to come aboard and come in and allow God to govern your entire life, and I hope that you decide to surrender like I did. Hopefully, you will keep going on, and more will be revealed. If you got something out of this there will be more that will be discovered. Stick with me as I continue to tell you the things that you might have to embark upon that you will need a way out. We're here today to bring you the living word of God. This was the 1st step I needed to do toward my redemption. It turned out to be the ONLY thing I needed the last 20 years!

God said in his word, "I have given you my word that it may go forth and you may go forth and preach the good news of the gospel." I remember the day I called my mother, I said, "Momma, I know you heard about the presidency of the United States being Afro-American. Barack Obama, the first Black president, and you would be as proud as his mother to see your son rise to the occasion and become president of the United States of America." Well, any mother that had a child who became president would be honored by the things of the world that they are involved in and that he reached that level and grew up to become the president. That's all good but you know, it's okay for a celebrity and it's okay for an idle figure of the world to bring forth the things of the world and that's greatness. And I said, "Momma I got one of the greatest jobs in the world!" And she said, "Well I don't know about all of that." So I said, "Momma I discovered that I have the most greatest and responsible job in the whole world that is preaching the good news of the gospel, preaching the word of God." And then I said, "That's more powerful than the president of the United States job. I'm representing the family that governs forces of the whole world. And that is the greatness of the word of God. I'm bringing forth, I'm removing the burdens and destroying yokes." As I continued, I spoke with conviction as I said, "God has called and I have answered. I can't do it any other way. Look you're going to have to understand. I'm going to step forward and I'm going on with it, you're going to have to make this happen, we going have to get along."

One of the things I can say for sure to my Momma. I said, "Momma, the greatest job in the world is preaching the good news. You see the devil don't want me. He don't want you to know that God's word will come to pass and someone is telling you these things will remove the burden and the yoke and destroy those things that will bring the whole world to its knees. And know that there is something greater than those things in Gods words. Gods' words are like dynamite. It can rearrange those things that were. And that's what dynamite does, it rearranges what was. So I say that to you so that you will know God is love." My momma said, "Boy you're crazy, you need to cut that out." So I said, "What? Alright momma, I got to please God. I'm for all of his righteousness and for all of his doings. (Yeah momma, I know I messed up when I was a kid, I didn't obey you. I know I didn't listen. I got into fights and trouble. I even got into things you got me out of, but I didn't know any better back then.)

Well...thank God. If you don't read the word of God, you can't know the word of God, and if you don't read the word of God and discover the truth then you can't do the will of God. And if you don't know better, you definitely can't do better with the wrong mentality. So I decided that I heard the call and I know that now there's a calling on my life. I couldn't adjust to understanding what it was that I needed to do. So what God did was he kept me isolated and he put me in a solitary place where I stayed by myself and obtained and studied the word of God (The short jail stint man) so that I would know the word of God. As preachers we have to be prepared. What we are preaching is the word of God. The key to it is that the word of God is all that you will need. But a lot of us still have resources of things that are irrelevant that we make seem like it's of major importance, and we have failed because we never made God our one and only source.

You see God is our source. He is our only source. He supplies our every need. The whole world can be against you, but God says go forward and preach the good news of the gospel. He said this is what you and I are supposed to be doing. So if you are not doing it then it's time that you realize that you come short. He said go out there into the entire world and preach the good news (of the gospel; diligently no matter what you're faced with) and you will know my fruits because you will know of my sayings and I said I will prepare a place for you. I continue to this day reading my bible daily and learning new things as I meditate. Do you know how many people are suffering from sickness, diseases, poverty, ill health of the world and never heard what God had to say about it? It's called Contrary Speech.

When the good news of the gospel showed up there were men that was sick but by their faith they were healed. They never claimed to possess the power but the power was with them that they had the wisdom God. Which is for us to have the word of God upon our lips to handle and encounter every situation that needs to be done. We bring all the things into capacity and the things and relationships of Gods way of doing things that will clarify everything that comes about the world. Saying that to bring forth the good news of the gospel is to remove the burdens and destroy the yokes of anyone that's associated with having lack, sickness, diseases, poverty, and ill health which are the things the world is encountering that they haven't found a way out.

But you have been saved. You have been saved and brought to a level of a way of escape when you have been redeemed, while the rest of the world is still suffering and trying to discover why they are going through the thing that's happening to them. Your belief system is allowing you to receive what so ever you believe. You have to believe it before you say it. So hoping you have belief and confidence in God's word, so you can bring forth the good news and see that Gods word goes throughout all the earth and not come back void.

When you come to that understanding you know that you have a calling on your life to preach the good news of the gospel. I could not imagine that my mother could see that there was a saying that our fathers seek and wait around to discover that the manifestation of man have posed the relationship that her son has received the anointment and the power of God in this life. In other words, I have a physical son, but it's nothing like when I stand by to see how long God comes in and pours out his spirit. Should I myself not know my son if my son comes forth like Jesus, and comes forth like the Messiah and comes through like Moses, Joseph, and comes out of the power to be able to preach the good news of the gospel. He should know the established word of God throughout the world.

Learn to ask and you will receive, seek and you will find, knock and the door will be open. You know what I'm saying! Well you really have to experience some stuff to have done wrong and you know that it's been washed away. Your sins are forgiven and God cleanses you and you will see that magnificent power of God, your personal relationship with God. It's something that will change lives and remove the burdens and destroy the yokes and strongholds. That's some powerful stuff if you ask me.

I hope that you will continue as we take further view in the life and understanding of the spiritual things that are the most important things in life for us to ever obtain. I discovered God has to do what he has to get you away from your family, friends and relatives so he can spend some time with you to show you some things. He wants to separate you from the world. God had to get me away from the world so he could deliver me back to the world. He had to get me out of the bondages that were surrounding me by influences, relatives, uncles, cousins, newspapers and anybody that has ever taught me or brought things into my life and the things of the world. Well, God changed all of that and he made it even greater. So I say that to hope that you understand that he had a bigger picture.

God is calling all of us. He said we have to obey him. But everybody is not interested in being obedient. Moses heard the calling of God. When God is going to prepare you to start letting you go forth into the world and guide you with the confidence that you're not going to change today after I assign you to go. He has given you the power and the ability to get results, love, and a sound mind. This is how you're going to know better. I'm going to make my word known to you but to them (the non-believers) it won't be known. This will be like the story of Noah, where no one believed God and they perished. God will manifest his word into existence throughout what is brought forth by the word. So with that in mind, there's a calling and many are called but a few are chosen.

I want to share how important it is to obtain his word in this relationship and to be obedient. And now, we have the victory over the world. You can live a productive grand life and feel grateful with great thoughts in your life. You will be like a magnet, which is the law of attraction. You will be attracting success, finances, and more business. You'll obtain favor in all of the above things once you learn the secret. It's the law of attraction.

Things happen in life...life has its turns and its twists and then we also come back when we have found out what brought us to where we are. I know the greatest success in my life is when I stay steadfast in the word of God and as long as I'm involved in the word of God, he will bless my hand in the things I'm attached to and in my relationship in the things I have trusted in him. He knows I don't make people my source. I made God my ONLY source, because he shall supply all my needs through his riches and his glory that he put in the glory and in Christ Jesus as it is written.

You know God made a covenant and he made a vow. You don't have to wait! Jesus is already risen! His salvation has been brought to pass and the lives and the believers. I've learned the word of God is so influenced the genuine seed of love is worldwide. I've talked to people from all walks of life and we all come to the understanding of God. And with that magic word of God, brings forth love. And love is God, and God is love and we all have gotten together as one mind, one body and one soul serving the same God.

So keep yourself immersed in the word of God because it's time for a change in your life and your mindset.

Chapter 10

Time for a change

I want you to know we have the power now and it's time. We have to change now and the change has to come on the world, but it's not the greatness. I'm not depending on a stimulus package. I'm not worried about sickness, because I bring sickness to its knees when it comes at me. Because I stand on the word of God and Gods word is sufficient. When God says contrary what the word is saying about sickness and disease, poverty and ill health, its God word that applies.

I hope hearing this has really made you aware of why I spoke of these things repeatedly that you will understand these things that I am telling you. I've experienced through the love of God, and what it is to walk in the word of God that I may share with you and forgive you no matter what. That's what I love about God. People put a for sale sign on forgiveness "Well I'll forgive you if you do this, or I'll forgive you if you do that." And they have the wrong mentality of thinking and I got to get even with you. I'm going to let you feel what I felt when you hurt me and now that's what hurts people. That's their job to hurt other people. Love supersedes all things. I remember every argument that ever happened and was resolved; it was because of the love of God. We decide to all walk in love and forgive. I can't get over this...I meet people that are still holding grudges. They are still walking on the other side of the street. They are still resentful of what happened and what someone else said. I've learned to forgive and forget. I've left those things behind and pressed on. Tomorrow is a new day, and I don't worry about tomorrow because tomorrow has its own troubles. God is supposed to be your source. It isn't your mother, father, your rich uncle, aunt, or your rich brothers and sisters. He will bring all the right resources you will need. I never wanted or need when I put him first. I never forget a time when I was sick and I needed about eleven thousand dollars. Man, I know the hand of God works.

I happened to minister to a guy and the guy said, "Man I have been out of the word for a long time G', and I tell you what...I sure appreciate the tape you gave me, It really explained the love and concern that you had that to get back in the word of God; even though I'm a Hollywood producer, I've produced big major films and movies...I'm going to talk to a friend of mine...I'm going to see if I can do something to embark upon and sow a seed in your life and that seed is twenty thousand dollars." I was so grateful; all I could do was nod YES.

I produced the 1st National Black Comedy Festival in 2005. I filled the house that night. I could not imagine what a great outcome it was. I didn't do this by myself. It was through the co-operation of other people. God brought all the right resources there in my life. I thank the brother that showed me the promotional game. He showed me how to sell over two thousand tickets, and people were embarking upon events and affairs that I produced, as I learned what it was to produce. My true trust was in God; that's how the root of it started. All this other stuff brought about that seed which was like the smallest seed. It was like a mustard seed and it produced the largest crop. And I can't believe that God showed me the evidence of trusting and believing in him, and got me out of debt. I got healed because I was sick and I didn't know that sickness brought about something of evil doing and thinking along with causing arguments, chaotic environments and complete confusion and disorder in my life. This lead to quarrelling and fussing on a lot of occasions. When I put that aside and stayed in the word, it was the word that got me through. When I was laying down sick on the bed, the guy who called me, he didn't even know I was sick until I told him.

That in itself was amazing when he showed up at my door. I had never seen this guy before. He came through the door and gave me twenty-thousands. My faith had been returned. He had given me twice what I asked for! That was God's love for me!

You have to decide to walk on the good side and you just can't do something good one time and expect to walk in light like that. You have to do it for a very long time, meaning the rest if your life (amen to that). You have to be committed to it and you going to have to do it for a long time until you get it right. And remember you can't cheat even if you wanted to. There's no cheating in this and you can't compromise with this you have to be fully dedicated. It's a lifelong commitment.

Remember, nothing just happens. There is a root to it and the number one root is fear. I can't stress that enough, as many men as there are out there who are having their hearts failing them, because of what they feared the most. There was a young man that I knew, and he died. He had open heart surgery and he said, "Man, you know I'm afraid if I forget or don't take my medicine I might die". We all checked back later to see the status. He had died of what he feared the most. See that's what Paul said, "What I feared the most came upon me." We'll talk at another time about this particular subject and we will find closure. When conversations were arisen, I was asked, "What kind of work do you do?" I explained how I minister to husbands and wives and guys coming in and out of the penitentiary and found out what I am discovering. I'm teaching the word of God, and what the word has to say about certain issues and certain things that bring the light on situations of people's lives. What I was finding out was how important it was that our conversations was starting out that we were talking about offense and fear, and we talked about these things that are happening right now. All that everyone in the world is wrestling with. Everything is the Law of Operation....

The bible says that we are the power that possesses the power that changes as long as you are alive. As long as you're alive, you are under the law. And there is a law of operation that brings forth death just like Jesus brings forth fruit to God. As we are the fruit, in other words the devil and the kingdom of operation in this kingdom bring forth sickness, disease, poverty, fear, and it brings forth that fruit which is bad fruit.

The law made sin the law that it is. He said if it hadn't been for the law, I wouldn't have recognized sin. The bible says that everything after is kind to all of them. All of these things will come to them. For all of them are alike the bible says. To all of them alike, all of these will come into them. Just like the guys all the things come onto them; dope fiends, the addicts, the drunks and the alcohols... all these things come unto them. And most of them will have to obey. It's a new law that as a young man these laws were made for those who break the law. But for all those who broke the law; only very few of them made it out.

I remember I use to ask my mom about people and she use to say, "That guy is low key, you would never know what he is doing. He drives an old car and wears regular clothes...he's not dressy or flashy, you know when that man is traveling and goes out of town he goes to the garage but he has his suit bag in the back of the car and he has on a suit shirt and tie and he goes to another town with all his diamonds and jewelry and goes and travels all over. And when he comes back he puts on the same clothes and drives that old car...and when he goes to the garage he has a Mercedes Benz, and he drives out of town and visits his daughters and his sons and family." But you would never know that guy because he's a smart and intelligent man, he was a man that was low key. You know to be low key is being incarnate that's the best man who ever survived this drug game, the man that kept a low profile.

A low profile is a man you couldn't ever imagine he was even involved in sinful worldly things, and he was the head man in charge. But that is an example in itself and the way of the world's thinking it was to bring us into where it's only these ways you can go to an institution, lead to death, or end up in jail and it's no one order, these things come together. But one thing is for sure you may start out in that path of thinking that is good and all sin is definitely good and it is designed to lure you in and capture you and bring you into captivity. Then you are being shackled and glued to it because you're being connected and not being able to get out. Very few of us are able to get out the game and realize that there is a better life and what is more important. We would rather spend our whole life chasing something that would never bring us a great profit, but troubles, trials, tribulations and adversity because it's no way you can live this life and have an involvement with God. Think of the way you had to indulge in order to stay alive and to stay out here in the streets and be able to know that people can owe you ten thousand dollars and you know you had no problem collecting the money. Others that would hear you were respected, and people would pay you and you would pay people in order to pay you. Are you with me?

All of these things are the general principles and laws that work in this business. Even the drug game was a law of operation and we made the law on our own terms. Even without rules and regulations that only applied in certain locations and in certain neighborhoods. But I didn't want to bring this to your attention for no reason. The reason is that there is a way out and there is an escape. But you have to make the choice! You are a free moral agent and you can make the choice. Hopefully you realize that what you do to others will come back to you.

The bible tells us that we are not to put stumbling stones against our brothers and get them to stumble. There is a light that needs to be shined and that shining on that light will bring darkness to scatter where there is light. The light is having the living word of God operating in your light then opposed to operating in sin, which is designed to kill you, and keep you in shackles and in bondage. It's that you need to keep yourself aware of this law. So you will not fall into this trap and be entrapped in this way. You can get out. Some things you cannot cheat even if you wanted to. When we often refuse what God wants us to do it is called rebellion. Who are we to tell the Lord what is best for us.

Rebellion is something that's very serious to be walking in. King Solomon lost his kingdom because of being rebellious, including his anointing. You can't lose the destiny that the Lord has for you. When you become rebellious it will rule your life. You will lose what God called you to do, because you let it stay in your life and you won't change. In those days, when you would lose the battle it was customary and it was tradition to take the best of the spoils. God said to destroy everything. He gives us signs and we are so rebellious when we can't even obey them.

Sometimes our rebellion is just like witchcraft. We must obey the voice of the Lord and do it from your heart. So plant love in your heart! Rebellion is the sin of witchcraft and stubbornness. Stubbornness and rebellion walks together had in hand. Rebellion and being stubborn and also walking in fear is harmful and detrimental to your life.

A stubborn person will be a rebellious person. How long will you let rebellion ruin your life, your family's life and other people's lives you deal with on a regular bases. You ARE risking losing your destiny because you keep rejecting the word of God so that you can feel good (your feelings are only involved) . Is it worth it? You tell me, ask yourself the question? If it's a good feeling, I really hope that you are enjoying it. Enjoy it and make it last a very long time because it can't stand up to the destiny of what our God has for us.

Rebellion means" I don't, I won't, I can't "change and it's these things that all produce negative vibes mixed with fear and it's supposed to be no fear here. Your pride gets in the way....

I don't need to change you. Tell yourself, you get fear and think I'm afraid to change. You have a rebellious spirit and say, 'I don't want to change. Laziness is a hindrance to change. I don't feel like changing.' We are not supposed to go by our feelings. Feelings will lead you to fear. Some people think it's too hard to change their lives or to change certain situations, 'It's too hard," so they say.

God requires much from you and you require much from God. Change is the order of the day! When people tell you they have an issue that's just how they are and they don't want to change because they love to have issues and fear These folk don't mind remaining stubborn and being rebellious. Being too lazy is sin, and some people, no matter how crazy it may seem or sound, are too lazy to even sin! Some don't even know laziness is a sin. That is a kind of sin that will keep you stagnant, meaning laziness will lead you right into poverty. Remember, when you're not changing, you're not growing. If you are lazy to change or you think it costs a lot of money to do this, then you're not willing to pay for much then you are on your way to poverty. And when we do this, we end up living an average life, right along with everyone else. (That's why you have to set high expectations for yourself and apply goals and morals in your life) It will appear as if we are doing just fine, and that's the big deception of it all.

We need to demand excellence from our lives. Nothing but the best is what God wants for all of us. We have to want it for ourselves and staying in the word will take you there and it will surely keep you there. Just use your key and your key is the bible. Your key is God's way, it's the only way, and it's the abundant way. Just like when we open our doors up with our key to the house, your key to start your car, we need to use the most powerful key which is our bibles to show us the way to have a sound mind over everything to communicate with the Lord. Pick a minute of the day to meditate and to ponder on it. That's God's way. God is love and love is God. Can you understand that? Well, I can understand it. Demand excellence of your way of life always. Jesus said the word I speak unto you is spirit. Spirit means the vital essence of animating force in living organisms. It's considered divine in origin. I can minister to your mind and your reasoning but if it doesn't get in your heart, you're not going to change!!

You have to take the step and put it in your heart and plant the seeds not the weeds. It's the word that's going to make you free as they say. The truth will set you free. Don't take the word away from your life. Without the word, you will definitely be confused. You will have fear, poverty, lack, sickness and disease. If you're too lazy to read the bible and too lazy to listen to tapes and too lazy to do things when it's time to try it out, it's fear, it's being stubborn and last but not least it's being rebellious.

Don't be too lazy to execute the word. How long will thou sleep O Sluggard? When will thou arise out of thy sleep? Yet a little sleep, a little slumber, a little folding of the hands to sleep. So shall thy poverty come as one that traveled, and thy want as an armed man? A naughty person, a wicked man, walked with a forward mouth. If you don't want to study the bible, don't expect to see your life success prosper in any area. Ignorance hinders us to change. The meaning of ignorance does not know, there's no understanding or no complying with any situation. Ignorance means" I never thought about changing". Ignorance is not an acceptable excuse to God. Some people don't know what God has for them on what their potential is and ignorance is not an excuse to God. I don't know. I didn't know or I didn't understand is no excuse to God.

It's not going to work when that day comes of judgment; God has giving us bibles: King James, bibles on DVD, Amplified versions and we still don't understand. There are a lot of people who thinks excuses will let them in, they're going to come to the gate and say, 'I'm righteous because I went to church or I sang in the choir or because I gave my tides.' Well it's not going to work. God is not interested in all these things you have done to try and make yourself look good and righteous. He is only interested in expecting Jesus and going in on the righteousness you accepted from Jesus.

God has given us his word and it is up to us to search it and study it and learn from it. You have to work out your own soul salvation. You are responsible for yourself and you must always except responsibility and do your part with the word, and working it out, you have to do that. You have to watch over your soul. Watching over your soul is teaching you correctly the word of God. Make sure every time you show up to church you're doing the right things in your heart, mind and soul.

Your soul should always be filled with the right stuff and to guard any other stuff that comes in and try to affect the way that you think. hat's watching over your soul teaching us one of the most compassionate things; you can do in the life of a person. God has compassion and he teaches us if we want to be taught it's up to the individual. If you nourish your emotion, you will become emotional. You don't have a word to stand on you're just emotional and emotional is fear. We can't let one crack of fear into our lives. You have to develop your emotions to move emotionless when problems come.

You also have to nourish your soul in every way. In a time of trouble if you depend on God's word knowing what you know, you will always have your victory with the word of God. No matter how hard it is, how bad it seems, he will never let you down. he will see you through. In times of troubles you will go back to what you know, no matter how it hurts, you're going to stand on that word crying if you have to but weeping will endure fro the night, but joy, if you keep standing will come in the morning. Your soul will now be nourished and in times of troubles you will be defeated because of your soul.

People are saying things in the bible that's not even in the bible, they're saying the words but Gods word can't be changed. Change is the order of the day you have to nourish your life with the word of God so when trouble comes you have something to stand on, but if you don't know any better, you can't do no better. I'm still growing because I'm changing but I bet you I'm not the same person I was twenty years ago, you know why? It's because of the word of God, and it's because I changed.

I'm not going to stop changing until I get to the perfect place. I've made many mistakes but boy I've surely learned from them and the learning part is the understanding phase. Now instead of going the wrong way I'm going in love's way; God's way because God is love. I will never be guilty in not loving because I will always walk in God's love. If I keep changing, I'll keep growing and I'll get to that place that will most likely please him and it will certainly please me.

A blasting explosion should take place in everyone's life. A sudden spread blast of knowledge and glory will take you out of your lack, sickness, debt and everything that needs to be blasted out. The anatomy is the act of dividing things or the act of dividing anything for the purpose of examining its parts. We can also divide life into pieces and divide life into steps. So we can examine each part, look at those parts and discover the things that we can do to make our lives much better. It's not hard to have the kind of life we all want to have. It's very easy. All you have to do is divide your life up and we can understand what we need to do. Words are so important in our lives. No one ever wants to deal with the beginnings of everything. Words are just like seeds, when we say words out of our mouths, we plant them in other people's hearts and heads. But when we say it out of our mouths it should come always from our hearts.

Our tongue is like a pen. It writes the way we think and the way we think will produce the emotions that we have or how we feel. How we feel will produce the decisions you will make in your life and your family's lives. The decision you make in your life will bring it to the point where it will produce the different actions that you take. Words will produce the way you think, the way you think will produce the way you feel, the way you feel will produce the decisions you make, the decisions you make will produce the actions that you take, the actions you take will produce the habits you create, and the habits you create will produce your character and your character will bring your destination in life.

You must change your character if you don't like your character. Then change your habits. If you don't like your habits, then change your actions. If you don't like your actions, then change your decisions. If you don't like your decisions then change the way you feel. If you don't like the way you feel, then change the way you think. Ultimately, if you don't like any of those things, then you better start changing your words and you need to do something immediately. Do you get it??!!

Make sure you change the influences and the images that are around you. There are a lot of things going on in the world at these times. People are out of work, people are homeless, the divorce rate is higher than it's ever been, and people are just confused.

Remember, words are just like seeds. Everything we know starts with a seed. Everything that we see in our life, things that we eat, started from a seed. When you examine this first area of words like you look at seeds, they are the beginning of things. They are the start of things, that's the place where things are started, where things begin with words.

Words can hurt you and if you don't recognize the power that's invested in words they might just kill you one day. Words will produce images, good words produce images, these same words will be used to cause influences and they also create catastrophes.

Words are very; very powerful. Human beings have basic needs, and everything starts with words. Acceptance knows that you're loved and that you're needed. Every human being needs to know that they are loved and that they are needed. That's called acceptance. Everyone needs to know that they are special and that they have their own identity. Everyone needs to know that they have security that they can be provided for, and they also can be protected. Everyone needs to know purpose that they are here to accomplish things in their lives.

Everyone needs to have acceptance, identity, security and purpose. If the seeds of life are not presented to children as they grow to teenagers as they begin to develop. Even in marriage relationships the results won't be good. Words can change a person for the good and for the bad. From being negative to positive, words can encourage a person to want to do better in life, words is the beginning. It's where we get our images, but watch very carefully and closely the things that you entertain and the images that you take in. Some things can be toxic for us and there are things that we need to eliminate from our lives and our paths. Sometimes you have to cut all ties and it may not be easy, but to save yourself, it might be the best and only solution for you. Everybody won't be with you in your time of trouble and everybody can't walk in your shoes.

There will be times where it will seem like a mission impossible, but remember everything in life is a test. It's like being a track star and trying to be the first to get pass all of the other competition or they will get pass you and reach the finish line before you. As you're racing, your aim is to win despite the obstacles you're faced with and even though the clock is ticking and you're running out of time, you see yourself reaching the finish line, you picture yourself being victorious and your desire is to win the race!

Chapter 11

Mission Impossible

It takes a burning desire and a strong drive to push your dreams. The idea is to never give up. Keep pushing forward, as I did and you will soon see If you learn from the life I lived and how the end result turned out, you can make it big too. Like the James Bond of Harlem, navigating through different avenues of success. As New York's Own Hollywood, the entertainment producer and promoter, business owner, and the man they call preacher man.

The greatest mastermind of a mission impossible will demonstrate to you how to incorporate manifestation into your life. What you think, what you speak and what you feel is very powerful. This determines where you are positioned in life.

So you have to be careful how you think. It is critical, you must think like a mastermind.

Throughout my life, I have steadily demonstrated the ways to walk on a path unlimited. I dreamed big, and when the missions were assigned, I carried them out. There were some obstacles along the way and rough bumps in the road, but I kept on pushing forward and remained diligent.

My life is like a mission impossible, ever since I was Lil G. I lived the life. I saw the type of money that would make you take a double-take, and from young, at an earlier age I had it all; the girls, the cars, everything. You named it, I had it.

I specialized in dealing with large amounts. I had all types of duffle bags stuffed with money. I traveled the world and went on exclusive getaways. I attended private parties, and became VIP status. I am amongst the elite, and I have been at the top of the who's who in names and this is the life some people can only imagine. As usual, they try to imitate that fantasy.

On the road to riches and the finer things, there were many missions encountered. As I witnessed what seemed to be impossible become possible. Nights where I was on the hustle, not sleeping, remembering somebody's always creeping and watching, while the haters clocking your every move. I had to do what I had to do to survive.

It was like being in a battlefield. I had to keep focused to stay alive and put some things aside and come back to return for it some other time. Late nights I was selling, watching my steps, and looking out for informers who were telling all and snitching. I couldn't let anything derail my mission.

I knew my position and took charge. Anything that seemed like a possible threat had to be nipped in the bud. So, at all times, I had my connects lined up so we could eliminate all the competition. As the word spread, and my name became notorious, I encountered constant friction because I couldn't be beat, and that turned up the heat in the streets. So I had to make some calls to handle hectic situations, and it left a lot of people with frustration.

I was placed in the position of power. I was running work and doing deals with people who were big time in the streets and the competitors couldn't take it. They was angry, they didn't want to see me getting all that money and taking over. They were trying to figure out how I was making it happen. Strategic moves were made like chess, while I always impressed and persuaded, my movement never faded.

I moved like a mastermind and everything I touched multiplied. When I was I was put to the test; I proved I was ready for this lifestyle. I was dedicated, I put in the time, energy and everything required for producing a chain reaction.

I was letting nothing get in my way. I was about my business and making my money. The haters couldn't stop my flow. The word was out about me, I was on to something, my business was rapidly expanding and it made people ponder. They were stuck wondering how I do it. They saw me from very young able to maintain, attract and obtain all the material things and they were amazed at times. They were in a state of awe, watching me step out of limousines.

I use to step out of limousines flossing in the hottest designs, my pockets were swollen and I was ready for anything. Spectators watched closely, and they were amazed.

People would come up to me out of nowhere, inviting me to show up at different events and they were curious to know all the details concerning me. There were rumors circulating. G'Money, who is the real G'Money? Man... I have people claiming to be me to this day!!

I was everyplace. I had marked my territory swiftly and they were wondering how I did it and didn't know all the things that took place to make it happen. And although, they may think they know the answer, but a lot of people don't understand, when you trying to accomplish your goals and desire to make something big happen, you can't take everybody with you.

You have to disconnect from some people, but there are some people that you must take with you and those are the people that will be there to push you to the next level. They place you in the position, where you need to be. Understand something, when you want to make it big in life, you have to have that mentality.

You have to see yourself being big time. And surround yourself with a circle of people who serve a purpose in the area you concentrate on the most. Keep yourself connected to dreamers. And don't be afraid to fail a couple of times. When you get back up, you have to come back stronger than the first time. There may be some setbacks, but the setback is for the comeback. So give it all that you got. And don't look back!!

You have to pursue without fear. You have to realize you can have what you want when you learn the manifestation through divine purpose. Then draw closer to the circle of the people you are affiliated with, having confidence that you will succeed in your every mission. Knowing it's not impossible, because you allowed divine order to take over the situation. You must believe it in its entirety that it will be yours and that you will receive it.

In any affiliation, when you desire something so strongly, to obtain it, it takes a certain strategy. The whole process of how you got from point A to point Z takes great effort and depending on the work you put in, it will determine the end results. Not only do you have to do researching and analyzing, but you have to also make connections with all of the key players involved.

If you want it as badly as you say you do, you'll stop at nothing...until you obtain it. The stronger your desire, the greater your drive and you have to keep your eye on the target until you get what you want. At that point, there may be more obstacles in your way and that's when it becomes a greater mission, and as you dodge all of the obstacles, you see what appears to be impossible become possible.

There is a mystery behind it for some. How did it happen? When it seemed like there was everything that could possibly block the vision in the way...well, I'll tell you. There is a divine force always in the mix.

A higher power is always present, which causes the impossible; to become possible. Nothing is too great for divine authority. All you have to do is believe in divine power and then divine order will restructure the situation at hand.

You see, during my negotiations and networking, I came across people who thought they had it all figured out. They wanted to do things their way and make more of a profit off of me and take more ownership of percentages that they were not rightfully entitled to. It would turn out to be more beneficial for them and less beneficial to me. You've got to be kidding me.

With my street knowledge and book knowledge, plus, through years of experience, if the numbers don't add up correctly, it's time to explore other options. So, a few people didn't make it to this present point, taken away with greed, thinking that they had me right where they wanted me. That's when they saw the light of truth. Never do anything out of desperation. It will get you nowhere.

When you make any business transactions, make sure you know what you're entering agreement into. Don't be easily persuaded by words that sound good and then when you sit down and analyze it, you see right through the whole scheme. Make sure you stay on point at all times.

Looking back, from where I was, to where I am now...Yeah it was a mission. From my first hustle, to going the legitimate route, man the 007 moments. How we had to go and get this money, the rent had to be paid, on the look-out, running through alleys, parking lots, and abandoned buildings trying to escape getting locked up.

Man, I remember getting chased down in the wee hours of the night... getting chased down by some punks. I made it out that situation, but it was a struggle to survive. The things I saw, when I had to console my close friends family after seeing them dying and feeling the emptiness build up and wear down this heavy burden on my chest.

I endured all the pleasures, pains and pressure of the street life for the love of money I risked my life everyday involved in that atmosphere. Then I decided to take a new route. I made a decision to go the legitimate route, and chose to follow the divine plan, instead of doing it my way and things got more intense. I started to see things quickly shifting all around me. More opportunities were presented to me and regained strength in areas I lacked in.

The mastermind was focused. Ideas started flowing rapidly; everything that didn't make sense to me became very clear. I was empowered and unstoppable. I gathered my thoughts together and started presenting proposals, discussing my ideas on how to manifest my vision, using the mastermind technique, hiring interested individuals...who assisted in the process, some who were not there for the long run. But, they did their fair share to make it happen. Then they vanished in the blink of an eye. Even though they had good intentions, everyone can't go where you go.

I was up late nights brainstorming, figuring out how to connect all the pieces like a puzzle. Then I had to dissect this project down to a science and do calculations like mathematics. I knew everyone that was added to the plate served a purpose but, not everyone needed to be there upon the completion, so it was time to do some subtraction. I had to minus all of the weak links.

I had to eliminate all those smooth talkers...those who talked a good one, but couldn't walk the walk. They sounded believable, but their actions showed me a different point of view. And talk is cheap. At the end of the day, this is business and there's money to be made, no time to play games.

When you dream, you have to dream big. And my vision is so big, I had to get a lot of people involved to make this happen. I also had to make sure I got the right people involved, otherwise, things wouldn't operate properly. It's like running a business, if you hire a lazy worker with no ambition and drive, he/she will slack on the job, and your business will suffer due to a careless worker and poor performance. You will end up losing clients and your money.

When you do business, you have to do business with reliable people. And make sure you're not signing a deal/contract with someone who is only out to jerk you in the long run and leave you with limited funds in the end. I explored all my options and continued to carry out my mission, despite the distractions, I'm a winner. Winners win in the end.

Then you have to watch out for the rats! The ones infiltrating trying to get in on what you worked so hard to put together. They smiling and scheming with everybody you know. How about they're making contact with all your connections Meanwhile, their intent is to sabotage your whole operation. They got a hold of the contact list, they showing up at different locations, and you don't associate with them on any level. But they try to get a quick payday. Not around here, it's not happening. That got shut down as soon as the word spread and their whole plan flopped.

I'm not surprised when I see certain things go on behind the scenes. Everybody always sees the end result, the glitter and glam... but nobody sees the blood, sweat and tears. All the work put into making the actual vision come to the light. The sleepless nights required to produce everything needed to create a powerful effect.

No one knows what you experienced to make it happen. They just see a pretty picture. The perfect lifestyle, but do they know there's places certain people can't enter or they won't come out alive. There's people in high positions that could just make one phone call, and make you disappear, then make it look like an accident. You could be in the wrong place, handling your business, and when you step out the door, BAM!!! Not knowing the set up was waiting for you right around the corner!!!

You have to protect what you possess. Guard it. Don't go running around being a show off. You see, when people see your rise to success, not everyone is going to be smiling because they wish you well. Some of them will be smiling because they want to take your place and might be trying to devise a plan to put you out of commission all together. So they could mark your territory as their own. So, you have to stay on point at all times. Never sleep on your opponent, cause if you even leave one opening for their foot to get into the door, it could be your biggest downfall.

On this mission, it's strictly divine order. Along with a winner mentality that makes it happen. As I said before, a loser never wins and a winner never quits. You have to already see yourself winning. In visions you must already picture and prepare for the greatest moment in your life. And watch the type of people that you are surrounded by. A strong minded man doesn't need to be guided by a weak minded man. If the strong follows the weak, he may eventually give up too, but if the weak follow the strong, he will learn how to gain the same strength the strong man possesses.

You have to be strong mentally for any operation to be successful. It starts with mind power. Do you believe that the impossible will become possible? Even if doors have been shut in your face and you have been told a million no's, who's to say that you will never get what you intended to receive.

If you believe in divine power, you will be enlightened and things will become new. You will have a new start, travel down a new path and live a new life. You will see things happening in your life that you never imagined. And everything in your life will flourish; everything that you touch will prosper and be successful.

People think that they can interfere with the flow of things and the way things are going for you. The main reason is because they want to be a part of it and feel power, but at the end of the day, if it's meant for you; you will have it one way or the other. GOD will intervene, and prove, that even if they tried to stop you from receiving it the first time, the second time around, you'll gain more than what was originally intended. If you put your trust in GOD, you will see miraculous results unfold in your life.

I had to make a decision, either to continue to do things my way, or to choose wisely, and look to a higher power. When I reached a point in life, where my unlimited self-started to project and manifest my inner thoughts and intentions. I knew that it was because I was witnessing the magnificent power of divine order and original intent.

If you observe my life story, out of all the things I had from young, look at all of the situations I encountered. I would think about the times that those things were taken away from me. It was because I was not doing it HIS way. So those things were removed so I could learn to focus on what was important, then I was able to receive more in abundance.

Now I don't lack. My needs and wants are fulfilled and there is balance and stability. I no longer am subjected to partiality in areas that are now made whole and complete. I am not subjected to the old mindset that dominated the world I connected myself to by my flesh. The disconnection from that environment, led to me becoming better established in business and all areas of my life.

You have the opportunity too, to see things reverse in your life. To notice the drastic changes that can occur and see the work of divine power interceding in your life, helping you to overcome the obstacles that have kept you prisoner for far too long. If you want to experience that type of change, believe in divine intervention, and you will witness the impossible transition into the possible.

All that you have to do is trust and believe in the divine power, then you will witness as everything unfolds. That's what happened in my life. As soon as I let go of what was and looked to what is, there was a drastic change in my life. I knew I couldn't turn back. There was no way that I could go backwards. I had to keep moving forward. I didn't look back to what was or how things use to be. All that I know now is how to move forward. I pushed myself to a higher plateau. But I am where I am today because of the divine authority. GOD leads the way of my path.

Some nights were stormy, and during my trials and tribulations, I couldn't see it then but when I was doing things my way, it's was God's grace that sustained me. When I was on a mission, somehow things always managed to work out in my favor, but then I watched things fall apart. I looked at my inner circle and I could see people who were being affected in different areas of their life, but I was still on solid ground. Even when things seemed broken, they stayed together and never completely fell apart.

I started seeing things in a different light. There's nights when I was out in the streets and it looked like I wouldn't be able to get out of some situations. That's how caught up I was. But then it all turned around. I lived to see the light of day and think about how fortunate I was to still be around, and although I was hit hard at times, when I fell...I got back up and returned even stronger. The setback is for the comeback.

I knew that if I fell down, I wouldn't stay down forever. You have to have the will to survive by any means. Giving up is never an option. Quitting is never a question and doubting yourself is never a thought. You just have to figure out a way and if you don't have a way, you have to make a way. NEVER ever think that you can't. Always remember whatever you put out is what you will receive.

Confidence is a must, if you don't believe in yourself, how will someone else believe in you? But when you have that drive and ambition, and when you're focused and pursuing your dreams, that's when the challenges come. Don't doubt yourself. Affirm your capabilities.

There were times when I fell down and I fell hard, but when I got back up I came back stronger and more determined to succeed. Some people might have thought that it was over for me. That I would never rise back to the top, but when you really want something, you won't stop trying until you get it.

I realized from a young age that I was destined to make it in life and be very successful. I knew that I couldn't let anything discourage me. I had a lot of challenging moments in my life, but I made it through the storm with a new outlook on life. The tough times made me strive to be greater and achieve better things. I took a lot of risks because I was foolish and blinded by the material world.

As I think about it now, I could have died in those streets. When I was on a mission and risking my life, it could have been my family that received a devastating phone call. At the time, all I was focused on was getting money and wearing the most expensive things that money could buy. I lived life in the fast lane; I got a thrill from living on the edge, getting high and being exposed to the exciting scenery full of beautiful women, and making fast money. I lived for that life.

I wasn't thinking about leaving that lifestyle alone. I loved every moment of it. I didn't care about the consequences I was addicted to it and I couldn't stop. I was fearless.

I was a gangster and that's all that I knew. When I was on a mission, anyone trying to get in my way would get dealt with. It was either you find a way to make it or perish. I wasn't coming out the victim, I was victorious.

I was living the life, so I thought, but when things started getting complicated; I realized there had to be another way. I mean I fell so hard, it looked like I'd never recover. It was a reality check to me. When I didn't have spiritual guidance, I was so caught up and although I had access to everything I wanted, I was still limited.

There was something missing in my life. But I was in too deep to turn back or question what I really needed. After experiencing all the things that I encountered, there was no way that I could turn back. I was so caught up. The world that I was living in, it seemed surreal. Sometimes when I woke up, I was in strange places, unaware of what occurred the night before. And this is the lifestyle of many that go the route I went.

I never intended to make the big transformation that I did or become the man that I am today. As I said, I was limited because I was doing things my way and living how I wanted to live. It was very clear that I would get but so far and it was only a matter of time the reality hit me. It's either God's way or suffer the consequences of being disobedient and living in sin.

There was nothing that anyone could tell me to change my choice of lifestyle. My mind was set already. But when things took a turn for the worst and I had no place to turn, I had a reality check. When the closest people to me became distant and had difficult moments in life, I had to see what I had become. All of the materials things gave me the access to all that I desired, but with great pleasures comes great troubles.

A man can have all that he wants in life and still not be satisfied. When you live the fast life, it's for the moment. Getting high, having your choice of sleeping with whoever you want to, and fulfilling all of your desires.

Think about the power of money. I had what I wanted on demand at the drop of a dime. All the materials things and all that wealth didn't mean anything, because I still felt emptiness inside. My soul was searching for a change. I needed to be redeemed. But how can a man get released from his sinful nature? I became who I was because of what I was taught and the examples that I saw in my life. My uncles and cousins and the men that showed me how to get money and introduced me to that lifestyle.

At the time, I didn't feel threatened. It was all that I knew. But as I was out there, I put stumbling blocks and obstacles before my brothers. I had no conscious of it because I had no spiritual base. I thought like a gangster and it was survival of the fittest.

Then I was awakened, when I accepted GOD into my life I had my answer, I knew what was missing. I needed to follow a higher power instead of all the men in my life. Yeah, they showed me how to get money and access to all the material things in life, but there is one key thing that they could never give me; eternal life. The path I was on before I converted my life was full of uncertainty, so many of my friends that ran with me never made it to see daylight, but I did...

I am thankful to be here today to tell my life story and I am blessed because some of my friends just vanished in the blink of an eye. I watched them dropped one by one. I remember it like it was just yesterday. The devastation took its toll on me. You see, once your eyes close for good, that's it, there's no coming back! But that's the chance you take, when the streets are calling and you're anxious to get those crisp hundreds in the palm of your hands. At the end of the day, it's not worth it. I know now, I risked my life but there is a better way,... God's way.

In order for me to get back on top, I had to do things God's way. The moment that I did, it was apparent to me. I was actually placed in a better position than I had ever been in during my entire life. .And all that was limited was without limitations. Doors that were once closed started to open up for me. People started presenting opportunities and proposals to me out of the clear blue. Without a problem, I got the chance to accomplish some major things in my life. I couldn't have done it, without accepting God and changing my lifestyle and my way of thinking.

I had to renew my mind. The impossible can become possible. Don't think that things can't happen in your favor, they can, but what is your belief system. Your belief system determines everything, and how you think. I realized from a young age that I was determined to make it and life and be very successful. I knew that I couldn't let anything discourage me. I had a lot of challenging moments in my life, but I made it through the storm. Stay focused and stay grateful...

I dreamed big and the manifestation of my thoughts and divine power elevated my success. Because of this, I went after everything that I wanted in life. I made huge accomplishments, but when you're making big things happen, there's always going to be some kind of hater lurking. They are watching your every movement and judging you based on their own assumptions!

There's people who have nothing better to do, so they sit around wondering what you did and who you did it with. They use all their energy trying to find out all they can about you. So they can paint their own picture. Then before you know it they twist the whole story around. You hear your name mixed up in situations and places that you weren't even in. Now how does your name get mixed up like that and you wasn't even at that location when the whole thing went down? It was a hater!

No matter what you have going on; make sure you KEEP a positive outlook on life despite the haters and obstacles trying to block you in life. Eliminate your associations with the negative people in your life and you will see drastic changes. You don't need to feel acceptance from anyone. God's love is sufficient and will suffice. Know that God will do amazing things for you in your life, just like he has done for mines.

All that you have to do is believe in divine blessings and let God into your heart. It is because of God that I am who I am today. I am a redeemed man. Truthfully? It would be impossible for me to have come this far without God and God's love.

God changed my life; he restored me and gave my life new meaning. There were people out there who hated on me. God revealed them to me one by one by name. Although my enemies tried to throw me off track by using hateful tactics, they were not able to succeed at their mission.

There are a lot of undercover haters out there; some of them will even pose as close acquaintances just to try to bring you down. But what God has for you is for you. I got past all the haters. Remember to be leary! There's always a hater some place close, so you must beware of haters!!

Every person that you meet in the world or that you encounter, whether it's through family, mutual friends, at the work place, in the streets or anywhere that you have exposure, has something on their agenda for you. The question is, for every person that you meet, what's on" their" agenda? What is their initial intent when they connect with you and establish a relationship with you?

It is imperative that you know what types of people are in your circle. Do you have haters amongst you, who you think are your friends that you can trust and rely on if times get rough?

Remember your P's and Q's on due diligence? When possible, do a background check on any new associates coming to your team. It will save you lost time and money if you find out that they embezzled at their last job or have a massive reputation for violence or a rap sheet longer than the Brooklyn Bridge!

Chapter 12

Haters

The first thing you have to watch out for when you're moving ahead in life is the haters. The moment that they see you rising to the top, their smile becomes a frown. They don't want to see you make it to too high of a level. That's when the competition comes into play.

What do haters do? Haters hate all day, they hate with a passion. They will do whatever it takes to stop you or delay your flow of things. They just want to keep you off track and make sure that you don't succeed. They are like sharks in a fish tank or crabs in the barrel; they will do whatever it takes to make sure you don't make it to the top.

Haters carry so much hate and malice deep within. Sometimes it gets to point where even if they have to be deceptive and smile in your face, while they pretend to congratulate you, they will at the same time they'll devise a plan behind your back to eliminate you. But smile, you know if a hater hates, you're doing something right!

Realize that you're placed in the right position in life and they want to imitate you and become just like you. Haters study winners. They become mad when they see your success. It eats them up inside, because they don't want to see you maintain a successful status.

Think about all the haters you came across in your lifetime. Now think about the tough times when things weren't going right for you. Know that the haters enjoyed seeing you down! Hearing a story about how things were falling apart for you. But the minute that you make your comeback, haters get afraid. If they see things working out in your favor, their next step is to figure out how to destroy your whole operation. They'll work through your family, friends and anyone close to your heart. It becomes like an obsession.

But no matter what, don't let the haters stop your flow! Let them see you moving forward, fearlessly. Continue to excel to a higher plateau. All in all, don't let your guards down. Haters want to catch you slipping; they want to see your world shatter like broken glass. And be able to say, "Man he fell off, I remember when he used to be..." So they could sit there, laugh and rejoice over your downfall. Yeah! Even go have a drink gloating over your mishaps. All the while wondering how they could mimic you and try to do it better.

If you want to obtain the best things in life, you have to keep your circle small. Always act like somebody's watching you and pay close attention to the people you let in your life. All the while figuring out what is their purpose for being there. Everybody should serve a purpose in your life. When you start paying close attention to everyone, you will see who's really there for you and who's not. You have to watch the actions and movements of certain characters. You could have a hater in your circle and not even realize it. But there are people who only come into your life to destroy you.

There are people in life who do not want to see you amount to nothing. Those who, if they had their way, you wouldn't even exist! That's how strong their hatred is. When people try to do anything in their will power to keep you down, that's a snake. Some of you have serpents amongst you and don't even realize it.

You got so called friends sleeping with each other's husbands/wives, and then smiling days later like nothing happened. Sometimes, it's actually over stuff that happened way back in the days. You know people hold grudges for years. What makes a woman sleep with her best friend's man behind her back. They try to convince her friend that he's a dog and he's no good for her. But she failed to mention what she took part in. A lot of it is hate.

There are a lot of nice looking people in the world. People hate on those people because one way or the other, they cannot look like them. They get jealous because of the attention they attract. These people become envious. That is no way to live your life!!

Haters also hate the "Pretty Boy". The man attracts all kinds of women because of his looks and swagger. Next thing he knows he is being set up and a group of thugs jump him! They beat him so viciously that they disfigured his face. They left him alone, helpless and badly hurt! There were so many of them, he didn't stand a chance! Sound familiar in your neighborhood? Proving there is more than ONE kind of hater!

Then word on the streets spread that he was beat down and left for dead, just because of his good looks? The man's genetics caused that? Just because is it his fault his parents had good DNA? What the bleep?!

Sadly, a lot of things that occur in the world are caused by hate. But instead of trying to stop the next man, you could use that same energy to better yourself. Stop worrying about what he got and what you don't have. If you stop hating on others, you will realize that you can obtain the same things in your life.

It's not impossible; you can have what the next man possesses. But when you try to bring others down, eventually, you will go down with them too. The more energy you spend trying to bring someone else down is wasted energy. That is time spent where you could figure out a way to have what you want in life without trying to destroy someone else's life!

People don't think that way. They see you looking good, and it's a problem, they start making funny comments like, "Who she think she is...I don't like her, I can't stand her." They don't even know why they don't like the person. If you ask, "Why you don't like her?" They won't even be able to answer the question with an honest answer. That's CRAZY hate!

They don't have a valid reason to dislike you. So they make up false accusations about you. Anything that would negate you and make you look like a bad person, just to make themselves feel good inside. You can never turn the truth into the lie. The truth stands.

A successful person is a winner. Even if you throw dirt on top of their name and their reputation that can never take away the fact that they are successful. You can talk about their drug use, their sex addiction and all the partners they had, call them abusive and say whatever you want, but facts are real.

Some people always try to focus on the negative things. They try to point out all of your flaws. That is also a form of hate. If you never have anything good to say, keep your thoughts to yourself. Spend your time and energy building yourself up, not figuring out how to bring other people down with hate tactics.

There's people in the world that spend years holding a hateful grudge inside and won't even speak to their own parents. They walk around holding hatred for the one responsible for giving them life. They refuse to open a line of communication! How does that solve the problem?

Those are the same people that end up needing someone to come to their rescue and expect everybody to jump at their command. They won't let go of the past and accept that what was can no longer be. There is no forgiveness in their hearts, so the hate lingers and they take that hate with them to their grave.

You have to let go of certain things that happened in your life and forgive the people that offended you and hurt you. Forgive the people that caused that pain in your life. Let go of the past and how things were before. Move forward, and prosper in life. As long as you keep hate, you are allowing yourself to remain stagnate, still stuck, unable to move to the next level.

There are a lot of families suffering from broken homes. There's a lot of hidden hate, family secrets and individuals that need healing. Mothers who resented their children because they had to struggle to make a decent living and provide for their children. Sisters and brothers who have malice for each other because of favoritism, feelings of lack and being unwanted.

These young adolescents grow up and when they become adults they carry a torch of hate. Brothers and sisters not speaking to each other for years, everybody doing their own thing and not once stopping to think. How can you continue to live like that? How can you remain to live in separation and division? There are people who are divorced today because of in-laws who caused havoc and created confusion amongst the families. They were filled with deep hate and did everything in their will power to destroy the happiness in the home.

A lot of it is generational. It continues to occur, unless someone does something to stop it. There has to be some kind of intervention. Someone has to speak out and someone has to keep the peace, love and unity. The youth need structure. If you don't teach your kids, the jail system will. If more people unite, hate would diminish.

There are so many different ways you can prevent and avoid being a hater yourself. If you sincerely wish others well and want the best for them, you will have the best things in life. But that's the problem with some people; they don't want to give words of encouragement. Once you can't even wish another person well, you allow room for negative thoughts. You have to avoid that. Think of all the good things that you can say about someone, instead of remembering all the bad things.

Even if a relationship turned sour, you don't have to hate anybody because you're no longer with them. Wish that person well. You show maturity when you are able to accept that things are no longer the way they use be, and if you look at it from a different perspective, eventually, you will find the person for you. But ,the more time and energy you spend hating your ex-man/woman, you provide more space for more hate to grow.

It's not worth being bitter; you start thinking of spiteful things to do to them and how to get revenge. Let it go. Turn those hateful thoughts, into farewells, and don't look back. If it's meant to be, it will return. If not, hate is not the solution, making progress is. The progress is moving forward, not looking back, letting go...maybe one day you can develop a friendship and look back and laugh. If you want to be in a better place, you have to let go of the hate.

Don't let the hate block your blessings. There are things that are meant for you and haters try to stop you from receiving it. But don't fear; just believe that if it's meant for you it will be yours. GOD works in the most mysterious ways. I believe that strongly and if GOD intended it for you, then it's yours. It's already done. If you know you got some haters around you, don't play into the hate. Continue to go with your flow. Don't focus on anything else.

There's so much hate worldwide. Love has grown cold and there is no concern for one another. Back in the days, people use to look out for one another. If they knew your aunt or uncle; they would have your back. If you got caught in a hectic situation, they would bail you out. If you mentioned a name, they would hold you down. Now, the mentality of the people is the exact opposite. You get into something and folks don't want to get involved.

The people of today are almost emotionless. They are so cold, and if you get caught up, you're on your own. If you're really in a bind and you reach out for help, they'll start avoiding you and evading your phone calls. When times get rough and situations get tight, you get to see who's going to be there for you in the long run. Not everyone has your back!

The hate is international; it's not a race or color thing. Everywhere there's war and corruption. All caused by hate. There are places where parents are afraid to send their kids outside, fearing that they might not return because of the terrors that go on. That's the only life they know. They live in a world filled with hate and they live in fear. Not a pretty picture for sure.

No one sees how hate works. It's like a chain reaction. Have you ever been amongst a group of friends and two friends have issues with each other and then the third friend now has some kind of issue with the person too. It's crazy because that person doesn't have anything to do with the situation. Yet, they get involved too and the whole situation is blown out of proportion and by the end of the day everybody ends up fighting and it turns out to be two against one.

What does that tell you? It's simple, the third party always had some kind of hidden hate and all they were waiting for was the opportunity to present itself. That's how a hater operates. They stab you in your back when you least expect it. They wait until your back is turned, so you can't see it coming.

A true friend is not going to strike you when you're already down. Situations like this happen far too often, don't think that's a friend. You can't call a person your friend if they hate on you on the low. That's a hater looking for you to slip, stumble and fall down. Haters don't have your best interest at heart. They focus on figuring out ways to destroy your success and leave you looking pitiful.

There's all type of haters in the world. They're at the job, in the club, in the streets, even in some churches; everywhere! You got to shake that negative energy off. Now, think about this for a second. You go to work to support your family and keep a roof over your head at night, right? But there are a lot of haters at the workplace. There are people walking around who have a high status. Like the managers and top executives that treat everybody else like the underdogs.

You know what I'm talking about... Mr. or Mrs. so and so...they come in strutting they stuff and act like they have an attitude with the world and because they have a high position at the job. They feel superior to everyone. You don't have to mistreat anyone or make them feel like they are beneath you. There are people in the workplace who fire people every day because of the hidden hatred that they have for them. You just can't go around doing that to people.

People have to feed their families! There are people, who have no other source of income but their day job. People who have hidden hate belittle them and make them feel helpless and defenseless. This causes fear to escalate when they are thinking about living from check to check just to make ends meet. Just barely making it and the person who has the power to make you unemployed and homeless is a threat to your future! That's because they see you as a threat to take their job away FROM THEM!

There's hate everywhere! Even amongst strangers... you can be driving an exclusive luxury car but living in a rough neighborhood where most of the people in that area can't afford to buy a car like that. But it's yours! You worked long, hard hours to get it! YOUR money paid for it! You shouldn't be afraid to drive your car in certain neighborhoods... after you worked hard enough to one day treat yourself to your dream car!!

And then after all the hard work and money that you saved up, a hater will watch you driving your dream car and despise you for that. They might I hate on you so much, until the point where you come back to a vandalized car. That's terrible. Unfortunately, that's what haters do. They will say stuff like, "Who he think he is?" Or make comments like, "I can't stand her, she think she all that!" And it's shameful that people don't know how to congratulate one another and want to see others have the best things that life has to offer.

The haters roll deep in the clubs too. You're going there to mingle and have a good time and meet a few honeys and have a drink after a strenuous week at work. You're not thinking that you're in a possible danger zone or that you might not make it out the club alive. There are no metal detectors involved so you feel safe. You don't know what type of territory you're in. See, the haters know that's their domain. So a hater will watch you like a hawk and target you like prey. Unaware, your focus and attention may be directed elsewhere, but you have to stay on point.

While you dancing and hanging out, you don't even realize that you're being watched. So you have to always move like somebody's watching you. Because chances are, they are. Somebody is always looking and people are always watching. Believe me, you need to stay on point and remain alert. Don't get up in the club and have so many drinks that you staggering while trying to hail down a cab. That is a sign of weakness. If a predator sees that, you can become easy prey all because of not paying attention to your surroundings.

You're up in the club and unaware that the haters got their eyes on you. Peeping your fancy chains and noticing your diamond rings and you being flashy and pulling out stacks of money and trying to buy out the bar. You are unaware that all along they're plotting. Their thinking, 'Easy target,' and then when you take off you realize; wallet missing, bank card stolen, credit card taken, your I.D. jacked and your last hundred pocketed and they got you just like that.

Then there are even some haters in the place of worship. You have to remember a church is place of healing and a place where you can go to get deliverance and just because a person enters a place of worship does not mean that they're sanctified. You have to be reborn again in order to live in newness and walk on a godly path. You're not supposed to live according to the flesh or let your emotions govern your life. But there are some people who are guilty of this act. They come in the church and they pass judgment on people and become jealous just because the Pastor has a good spiritual relationship with fellow members. That adds resentment into the pot.

Meanwhile, what they have to remember is that a Pastor is a spiritual father, not a personal problem solver. They want all of the Pastor's time devoted only to them to solve their issues in their life, but they have to remember a Pastor must be the spiritual father and lead all of the people in the congregation. It is the Pastor's job to act as a vessel to keep you in connection with the heavenly father and the spiritual father will guide you, pray for you, and pray with you.

When you enter into the house of praise with a hateful attitude, how do you expect to be blessed? If you want a blessing you must first let other people get blessed first. You can't criticize your brothers and sisters who are in the need of healing just like you.

And another thing that goes on in the church. One cannot try to challenge the man of God. God's word will never pass away. It is written and it stands until the end of time. Some people try to challenge the Pastor. Don't you know he's teaching you the word of God? The pastor has extensively studied the bible. He is giving you spiritual food to guide you and assist you in finding salvation and being redeemed so that your soul won't be lost.

People have their agenda's all mixed up. It's time to learn how to eliminate hate. You don't have to worry about what the next man got and why you don't have it. You need to learn how to get what you want in life without degrading other people to make you feel good.

It is time for a change and the change is now. It is time to stand up and stop the hate. The hate is widespread and gone way too far. Having built up hate and animosity for one another is no way to live.

Take a look at the schools for example. Some children are afraid to go to school because of bullies bothering them. They are there to learn and get their education, not to have fear that they'll be beaten down on their way home. It's gotten way out of control; there is so much violence, hate crimes and incidents that have occurred that kids have to walk through metal detectors and carry guns just to feel safe. It's all a vicious cycle!

From a young age, these kids become accustomed to living in a war zone. Either they adapt or die mentality. This mentality becomes the NORM. No one uses preventative measures or tries to deter the youth from going that route. Instead society promotes it. Society makes it look acceptable, and harmless. Then when the death rate increases due to teen crime, they decide to speak out about it.

It shouldn't even get to that point. Why does it have to get that far? Here's the REALITY part. If the youth continue to live the street life, continue carrying guns and having neighborhood turf wars and shoot outs, there is only three ways it's going to turn out. They will get locked up and be incarcerated. And will have to start writing letters from jail and requesting commissary. Or they WILL get shot down and end up in a sealed body bag where their parents will have to identify them or they will barely make it out alive to tell their testimony only for them to go out the next day and risk their lives again! I know. I was ONE of them once.

If you think about it, this type of aggressive behavior and war mentality is incorporated into everything: video games, television shows, music, movies, magazines and just about every form of mass media you can think up. Unfortunately, the youth soak up this negative information like a sponge because they have unlimited access to different forms of corruption and it all springs from hate. Some individuals glorify gun usage, but where are the leaders that will stand up and lead the youth to a better tomorrow? The youth need positive examples and role models to guide them so that they won't go down a path that leads to destruction. They need to be taught to work hard for what they want in life and not to envy or hate on a person who has what they desire.

It's not only the youth that have these issues. There are adults who act childish and still have an old mind set. They're still carrying on like they did when they were an adolescent. Some of the youth of today are witnessing this behavior and following the wrong individuals because they are being misguided by people they look up to and want to be like when they reach adulthood. Again, been there, done that!

Sadly, some of them don't make it to adulthood. They were never taught to have structure and where there is no structure; there is room for destruction and failure. Incredibly in some cases, there are youth who do have guidance and positive influences in their life but because of the hate, they feel they have to fight to survive and defend themselves anyway to make it in this world. If they don't defend themselves, they will be labeled as weak and get treated like punks. There are a lot of good kids that get caught up in situations where they end up at the wrong place and at the wrong time. It's the old story:

it's all because of the company they keep or the type of characters they are surrounded by in their environment.

If the youth of today don't continue to have good examples of role models, they will become subjected to following what they see. There are so many forms of ignorance. The more that society promotes it, the more chaos and havoc it will create. Something must be done to break the cycle and create a change for a better tomorrow.

There's so much hate in the world. Have you ever felt somebody eyeing you down with the look of hate? It's like the look of a hungry pit bull ready to rip through your flesh. Haters got nothing better to do with their time or their energy. They just hate. When they see you doing your thing it irritates them. They don't want to see any light shining in your direction. Their faces always look the same too. Just plain MEAN!

But you can't let haters get the best of you. Don't let anything get in the way of you making it to the next level. You have to look at it like a board/video game. I say this because when you play any type of game, there is always an obstacle or an opponent trying to prevent you from making it to the next level. Their job is to make sure that you never make it to the next round.

They are there to suffocate you and block your progress and will do their best to keep you ungrounded so that you are no longer in a position to recover from the attack. They like to catch you when you least expect it so when you're caught off guard, you will be defenseless.

There are a lot of people in the world who have had some kind of experience with a hater at some point in their life. Even if it was not direct, hidden haters are more dangerous. An individual with hidden hate can be vindictive and conniving. But you have to realize something. No matter what, a hater can't stop you from succeeding in life.

A hater can't stop your flow and a hater can't block your blessings. The only way that can become possible is if YOU believe it or become weak and let it happen. You have to learn how to diffuse the hate. Know that when a hater throws out that negative energy, you can turn it into a positive. You don't have to acknowledge any of that bad energy because it's not beneficial to you and it won't take you any place. Make believe it doesn't even exist!

Don't even start trying to figure out what people think about you and wonder why they don't like you or hate on you. If you try, then know that you will get lost in the matrix. If you know that you're special and that you're already somebody, no dirt thrown on your name will bring you down. God will lift you up and keep you on solid ground. So smile ☺

I'm here to tell you, let the haters hate and keep moving forward. Bless those that don't wish you well. That's right... I said it. You see, when you bless those that persecute you for no reason, your blessings will multiply. Don't give energy to negativity. Realize that you're better than that and know that no weapon formed against you shall prosper. The haters can lie and ridicule you and say whatever they want, but they can't touch you.

When you start putting your focus and your energy on positive things, you will be surrounded with positive energy. You have to elevate your mind and renew your mind set. The time that you spend worrying about somebody else, that time could be used for other things. For example, to brainstorm, create new ideas, and push your dreams. You can be a very powerful and influential person in life, but you have to leave the haters behind!

There are people in life that never pursued their dreams because they LET the haters stop them. These women and men had dreams that were waiting to be brought to life and manifested into reality. Then a hater stopped their flow and left them in a paralyzed state mentally, physically and emotionally, but it's time for people to reclaim their territory. It's time to rebirth your dreams and it's time to manifest what is meant for you.

Do not get discouraged and do not think that it's over. A survivor makes it in life because they have the will to survive. No matter what they encounter, they refuse to give up. They have a vision; they see themselves making it. They picture the end result. They believe that they will not perish and they hope for the best outcome.

If you've ever been affected by a hater in a negative way, it's time to make a change. It's time for you to reconstruct your life and push forward. It's time for you to tap back into those dreams and awaken them. If a hater stopped you from achieving something in your life, it's time to restore what they took away. If you believe that you are not where you are meant to be in life and you got delayed because of a hater, it's time dream again and it's time to live.

Remember, you are what you think you are. If you believe that you can't make it, then you won't. But if you picture yourself being victorious, despite all the odds, you will succeed and nothing will get in the way of your success. Not phony friends, lovers, relatives or anyone in your close circle.

What is your belief system? I look to God as my source and my strength for everything. If you will trust and believe in God, you will watch every hater vanish from your sight, your path and your thoughts. Their negative effects won't be able to interfere with anything concerning you.

That's what I experienced in my life, when I encountered haters; God intervened and as time passed by, what use to be a situation was no longer an issue. God removed every person and everything that wanted to deny me of what God had already given to me. If you will open up your mind and allow yourself to become a believer, every harassing situation will be rearranging.

Don't be afraid to stand alone. If you have to be aloof and distance yourself from certain people, then do it. Bring your mind to a new level. On this new level, you have to incorporate a new way of thinking. You can't think about what was, you have to accept what is. Confess that in the state of what is, you have completely disconnected yourself from what was and all of the things that prevented you from making your mark.

If you know that you have so called friends that are jealous of you, you don't need them around. The type of associates who bad mouth you and laugh it off like it's a joke. Take it seriously. WHY do you want to associate yourself with people who don't have your best interest at heart?

You have to recognize a hater. If a person is posing as your friend, watch their actions. Now either a person will congratulate you, compete with you or push you forward and help you to where you need to be in life. Some folks don't like to see too much happiness, that's when the hate starts brewing. They don't understand how you got successful. You will know if someone is genuine or not. It's all about their actions. If you got a girlfriend/boyfriend who's not supportive of your dreams or always tries to stop you from fulfilling your dreams and makes up every excuse as to why you shouldn't follow your dreams, wake up! That's a hater too! Don't FOOL yourself!

The more that you allow a hater to have a negative influence on your life; they will shatter your dreams, sabotage your plans and bring you down. If you're envisioning obtaining all the things in life that you dream of then you need good people around you. The ones who are going to motivate you, be supportive of your ideas and help you to build a foundation.

A lot of people fail because of the company that they keep. There are times when you must do the process of elimination. You must do an evaluation; look at the people you are surrounded by. It doesn't matter if it's your family, friends, lover, whomever. What is the connection they have in keeping you grounded and on the right path? You don't need to remain connected to a person if they're going to lead you in the wrong direction and bring you into the wrong path.

Misery loves company, but it's up to you make a decision to be miserable too. You don't have to involve yourself if you don't want to. It's all about the choices that we make in life. Don't point the finger at anyone or play the blame game, just look at yourself in the mirror. If you allow any type of behavior, then you are at fault. A person will only dish out what you accept.

There is a process you must undergo if you are surrounded by haters; you must release that negative energy and delete them out of your mind. If you want to see results, you can't hold on and you can't look back. In the biblical scriptures, Lots' wife looked back and she turned into a pillar of salt. That is profound. Now think about how your life will be impacted if you're connected to negative people who don't want to see you remain on solid ground. Those types of individuals will use every method to destroy every plan you ever had.

What you possess is the greatest gift; your mind! Use your mind power and your abilities to its highest capability. Don't give up the fight, don't believe that it's over if you fall, get back up. Rise and stand tall. Show those haters they can't stop you. Press on. Let them see that they can't hold you back any longer.

Your permanent state of mind should be filled with love, happiness, joy, excitement, peace and tranquility. You need not concern yourself with things that are not conducive to benefiting you. Free yourself from the captivity of the haters and be the best that you can be.

A hater is just as bad as a nagging woman, causing confusion, there's never a peaceful moment. All that you feel is uneasiness and an urge to find a way out of that situation. You might wonder how and why did you ever get involved with a person who caused you so much stress and sometimes bitterness? But just like a hater, there's a nagging woman somewhere, and at first she might appear to be loving, sweet, sincere, and trustworthy. Until, you meet the other side of her, the nagging side.

Think about it realistically, if you knew that a person was going to walk into your life to give you trouble and cause a bunch of unnecessary things to occur in your life, you would avoid them right? If you knew a person was a hater and always hating on people because they made more money than them or hating on a friend with a better boyfriend/girlfriend, who did more for their friend, then their current relationship, you would be suspicious of them right?

And eventually, you would get tired of the all the drama, just like a nagging woman; drama.

If you could spot trouble from a mile away, you would make a detour and go in another direction. You know what I discovered though, some people love drama. They live for it, like it's exciting to them seeing people get rowdy, but you can't let people get under your skin. It takes its toll on you after a while if you get involved in all the mix up.

Avoid all of the unnecessary drama; you could be entertaining something better with your time. Instead of getting caught up in all of the confusion, in comparison with a nagging woman, who wants to be a part of something that is not productive. Who wants a nagging woman? No man that I know.

Chapter 13

The Nagging Woman

Now, let's touch on a subject that affects men on a daily basis and this is something that every man can agree with. For all you women...PLEASE don't get offended by what I share with you. This information may be helpful to you and actually save your relationship if it's on the rocks. Take my words into consideration the next time you meet a new man, or for the man you're already with.

If it's one thing a man can't tolerate, it's a nagging woman. Now understand that nagging, whining and complaining will only lead to making a man frustrated. And just how much of it can a man take before he takes off and explores other options??

Too much of anything is no good for you. Seriously, a nagging woman is definitely not a good look!

Here is one example:

Abraham Lincoln had a wife, named Mary Todd; they were married for 22 years, until his assassination. She use to yell and scream, and as a result it caused Abraham Lincoln to withdraw and walk away from the relationship. Constant nagging and complaining becomes tedious.. it will make your mate want to walk away or find a way to get rid of you.

There are powerful men who found more success after divorcing their nagging women. What does that tell you? A man can be more productive and successful in life, once he eliminates all the problems in his life. A man needs a strong woman by his side, one who is supportive of him. Even if he fails at something, let him learn by his mistakes.

A man doesn't want to be dictated to and bossed around like your his momma. He doesn't want to come home from a hard day's work and hear you complaining about something petty. Something that can be avoided, it's not even an issue and what does the nagging woman do? She creates a chaotic environment.

Confusion equals to stress. A man wants to hear, "okay baby I understand you had to work late," not, "You a liar, I know you cheating! I called you mad times and you wasn't picking up my phone calls, who you was with? Who is she?"

Some women have the tendency to accuse too often. Remember you have to have proof. If there's no evidence that he's cheating and you're just basing it off of an assumption, you're doing a disservice to both you and him. Getting into an unnecessary argument because you believe he might be cheating, but you might be wrong. And if he's really NOT creeping, its things like that which can make him want to explore other options.

Now the black women get mad when brothers decide to date out of their race, but they shouldn't. Just take a picture of what is going on around you in the black community. The black man already has to face the challenges of life's obstacles thrown at him. He's already stereotyped as being a poor, uneducated thug, with no morals. He's falsely labeled as a person who robs for a living, drinks uncontrollably, does drugs, and lives a life of crime.

Society views the black man in a very negative light. They see the black man as a sex fiend who makes bastard babies all over the place and won't take care of them. Then the court system is forced to step in and make them pay child support. The black man is already up against a conspiracy the moment he's conceived in his mothers' womb.

Don't get anything twisted. Black women are built strong. They are queens and goddesses, but they have to have that mentality. Nine times out of ten, when I've discussed with brothers why they made the switch to go outside of their race, they had similar answers. The sisters were putting them down and putting too much pressure on them. They were not being supportive enough, and they were tired of dealing with aggressive, arrogant and ignorant behavior.

Save that aggression... a man can't deal with it. If you knew what he was thinking and the thoughts running through his mind, you'd put all that to the side. You need to realize, if you want to keep that man in your life, don't do things that will make him want to get in the car, drive down the highway and never come back. Even worse, stuff you somewhere where you'll never be found or heard from ever again. Relationships of a volatile nature tend to wear you down. Then everything deteriorates and it destroys the relationship. It can make love turn into hate.

Who wants to be going back and forth? Nobody wants to hear noise and encounter ruckus every time they turn around. Then you wonder why you can't reach him. Did it ever occur to you that he's trying to keep his sanity and he turned his phone off to avoid any further confrontation?

Women worry about the other woman too much. What they need to focus is on how you treat that man. Are you respecting him, or are you treating him like he's your son. There has to be a level of respect, even during a disagreement. If you're worried about another woman stealing him, you shouldn't.

Always remember, the competition that's out there don't matter. If you are treating that man right and being supportive and understanding, instead of nagging, complaining and accusing; he will realize the good woman that he already has. He will learn to appreciate what's already at home and won't be compelled to go searching.

When a man strays away from home, it can be for a number of reasons. There is so much temptation out there in the world. He can have the most beautiful woman alive and still start exploring other options. That's because of the lust and temptations of the world, he might have a good thing and ruin it, because he was too eager to romance every good looking woman in sight.

But there are some men who are capable of being monogamous. REALLY. But one thing that will destroy a relationship is accusations of mistrust. There has to be good communication in any relationship. Confusion and arguments is the recipe for disaster. Make a man want to rush home! Not provoke him to rush to the liquor store or the weed man cause you done stressed him out and driving him crazy ranting and raving with the same antics.

All that commotion causes too much friction. Living in the same house with a person and going days without speaking. Or because a woman is mad at her man she'll cook herself dinner, but won't leave him anything to eat. It gets tiring and eventually, it will make a person try to figure out a way to get rid of you.

Be cool, calm and collected. Even if you suspect something isn't right, don't go throwing it in his face. Because the more a woman nags, it takes a man closer to the pressure point and pressure bust pipes. So be mindful of your attitude and your demeanor. Remember that saying, "You get more results with honey than you do with vinegar." It's the truth. A woman can be one of the most beautiful women in the world, but if she has a forward mouth and likes to created confusion a man will leave her. He will seek his escaper in a state of desperation and he will not return.

Be mindful of your attitude towards him. The role of a woman besides her man is not to control him and dominate his every move and vice versa. A man don't want to feel like a woman is acting like his mother or making him feel like his is a prisoner and subjected to answering to a warden watching his every move. If he leaves the house and walks to the corner store, he doesn't want to feel like he's on house arrest, and can't go beyond a certain mile radius. Point blank, if you want to keep him in your life, keep doing the things you did to win his heart.

When you first met him, I'm sure you wasn't cussing him out and fighting and fussing and always complaining. Now don't get me wrong, not to say that these things don't happen in a relationship, they do because no one is perfect. But the two of you have to learn how to get past the fussing and fighting to come to a point of mutual agreement. Those moments where there are disagreements is supposed to bring you closer with your partner. It's not supposed to be a continuous situation that destroys your bond you made with one another.

Broken relationships need a foundation. You have to be able to build with a person. What do you want to accomplish and where do you see yourself with the person you made a commitment with? Just think about it, when you first meet somebody, you're not going to show them all of your flaws. You want to make your best first impression and you don't want anyone to think anything negative about you or say anything bad that would defame your character.

In all reality, you already know what type of individual you are, but you're not going to show any signs of being jealous, argumentative, problematic and quick tempered. It's all about your presentation, which keeps a person interested. The energy you project can bring about a negative reaction or a positive one.

Negative energy in relationships puts strains on relationships, people can't think straight. They go to work frustrated and start looking for a way to vent. If a man is caught up with a troublesome woman, he'll search for an outlet of security, where he feels comfort and momentary happiness. It'so important that he can get temporary relief and take his mind off of the situations at home.

A troublesome woman is like a thorn in your side. The piercing is deep and overwhelming, and it's something that's extremely unbearable. It's like a headache that just won't go away. It just keeps coming back!

As a man, there comes a point in time where you have to find a solution when facing those types of issues. It should not be through the act of violence. So many brothers are behind bars for situations where they continued a relationship with a nagging and argumentative woman and end up snapping one day. This is after being tired of being ridiculed and being treated like they were inferior. And when emotions and egos are affected by the power of words, somebody could get seriously hurt or even killed and it's not worth it.

You have to know when it's time to remove yourself from that type of element to prevent those altercations from occurring. Don't let it get to a point where she got a black eye and you're in handcuffs and she on her way to the precinct to get a restraining order. These things can be avoided. All the going back and forth is unnecessary. Remember the key... there has to be a level of respect on both ends and trust as well.

How can you be with someone you don't trust? Think about it logically. HOW can you love someone that you don't trust? Then you go to your friends and family and dog them out in one breath and be in-between the sheets saying, "I love you," in the next. That's not how love operates. If you love someone you not going to be stressing them out and making them not want to even be around you. Loves doesn't created confusion and make war.

People use the word love loosely, but do they know what love really is? Love is powerful and not to be taken for granted. If you love that man, don't nag, don't fuss, don't fight, stop complaining and learn to show love by your actions.

Realize that fussing and fighting is not the key. That will make a man resentful. If you want to know the answer to something, making assumptions will only make matters worse. DON'T listen to what your friend said, "Oh girl you know he creeping, I just saw him and so and so down the block, at the bar last night, kick him out! Kick him out girl!" If you listen to the wrong advice, you'll end up alone. Especially if your GIRLFRIEND is now dating him!

If you want answers, then watch the signs around you. Go by body language and actions. And remember, if a person wants to do something, they will do it regardless if you argue and fuss and fight with them.

It turns a man off when he has to deal with a nagging woman. That is why men try to avoid women who nag. If he doesn't get along with you, why would he want to be with you long term? There has to be a sense of growth and stability. No one wants to share a lifetime with someone who is a constant complainer. There is no future in that. It always end up the same way, starts out good, things is going smooth for a couple of days, and then everything blows up and explodes like an atomic bomb.

If your life fits this description as mentioned earlier, you need to do some self-evaluation and find a solution to resolve the problems in your life in a way where it will be beneficial and corrected without leading to unnecessary situations that will provoke a person and cause drama, stress and complicated circumstances.

For the women out there, if you know you have a history and tendency of being argumentative, that's something you need to correct. Just because the last man dealt with it, don't mean the next man will tolerate that behavior. Your attitude might chase away a good man.

You got to learn to let go of that mind set of hostile behavior towards your mind, if this applies to you. Not only will it keep peace in a relationship, but it will eliminate the excess baggage that comes with some relationships. Now there are things that cause the ongoing chaos to occur. There are things that need to be avoided. If you take my advice and are willing to learn from what I share with you, it will be beneficial to you in the long run.

The key factor to remember is to keep the love flowing in the relationship. Find ways to renew that bond between one another and try to prevent shouting matches. There should be other ways to communicate with someone. If it comes to a point where you feel like you're about to explode and need to let off some steam, it's best that you take a walk outside and get some fresh air, or try talking to someone who is level headed and will calm you down.

Change the subject, if it looks like a conversation is leading to an altercation. Try to express yourself without getting irate. Listen to your tone of voice and avoid tension. The way that you speak can provoke arguments, so make sure that your mannerism is not aggressive, and don't be too pushy.

Don't use forceful tactics, it will only create rage. If a person doesn't want to be bothered, give them some time to get their thoughts together and cool off. Trying to question or reason with an angry person only does harm.

Keep in mind, what arguments and yelling and screaming can lead to. You stand the chance of losing the person altogether and if things get out of hand someone can hurt and end up in the hospital.

There are lots of cases where somebody ends up getting hurt over an argument and over what somebody said, but those are only words. People say a lot of hurtful things when they get mad, but then it's too late to take back the words. You have to watch what you say to people.

Keep the relationship healthy. Instead of breaking up with a person over stupidity, learn how to forgive and accept the fact that people make mistakes, but you can move forward still without hurting each other. You can still get past difficult situations, but you have to know how to let go and learn not to keep bringing up stuff from the past.

If a person makes a mistake and you tell them you forgive them and then the two of you have a disagreement and you start bringing up old issues, you're back to square one. Avoid chaos.

Chapter 14

10 Things to Avoid

There are certain things in relationships that should be avoided. So I've compiled a list of ten things that should be avoided in a relationship. Hopefully, from my advice and information I share with you, you'll get the message behind it and you will learn all of the warning signs and take heed from what I tell you.

Warning sign #1-You realize you're involved with a person who has an overbearing personality. You find that 85 percent of your time spent with them they're nagging, starting arguments and fighting over nonsense. They're known for being quick tempered and irrational; and nothing gets through to them. Your words just go in one ear and out the other. Their attitude is always nasty, you don't know if you're going to get a stink facial expression or the cold shoulder, and they walk around careless, acting like you owe them something.

It irritates you to the point where you're tired of biting your tongue, but you try not to lose your cool until they provoke you to point where you are ready to do something crazy. All of your buttons have been pushed and you're ready to go ballistic and take it to the streets.

Have you ever been involved in a relationship with an overzealous person? Those type of relationships where it starts off like this, "Where you been at? Ugh uh...Why you had to work late? Who you were out with?" Well, usually if you start hearing these types of questions, it's in your best interest to proceed with caution.

These type of conversations start up at the most inconvenient time and it doesn't just stop right there, it's an ongoing thing. As it escalates you use up all of your time and energy, until you're left frustrated.

There are certain patterns to watch out for, the major points to remember. Again, watch out if you hear the words, "Where you been at? Who you was with? Why you had to work late? Why you ain't answering my calls? Why your hair look like that? Why you smell like that? Come here let me smell you. Have you been giving away my stuff? I don't know if I can trust you."

All of those words are key signals that you need be careful with what you've gotten yourself into. After a while you will feel confined and evade the conversation, so you won't have to give any explanations. There are a lot of people who have insecurity issues and that take its toll on any relationship.

Before you know it situations get out of hand and somebody ends up with a black eye, stabbed up, or shot. It doesn't have to get to that point where the cops are called, and it turns into a domestic violence situation. As you already know, getting locked up and doing time can be avoided. But you have to realize how those situations come about.

Most of the times, you hear about men getting locked up over beating up their women. And in most cases, these couples have a violent history. It's bad when the neighbors can say, "they're always yelling and screaming and fighting all the time." Eventually, the neighbors get tired of hearing all of the bickering and noise, so it becomes a habit for them to call the cops and put you on blast.

In the court system, there are lots of cases where women file reports on their boyfriends and go to get orders of protection when they are trying to get out of an abusive relationship. It shouldn't have to come to this point. If a woman wants out of the relationship, it's time to move on to somebody else.

Understand this, all of these things spring from control. Remember this key point, its control of your mind, body and soul. But you have to stand up and refuse to stay in a situation that is not suitable for you. The only way you will continue to have issues and be unhappy is if you stay and allow things to remain the same. You have the power to walk away.

As I said before, there are certain patterns to look out for. You have to remember the key points. Another key point is this, avoid mind control. If you hear certain words like, "You can't wear that dress; I don't want you wearing those shoes. You can't have that friend, and you can't go to that party without me. You can't work at that job," All of those words are forms of control.

Once a person has your mind, they have your body and your soul. So you have to start recognizing the patterns and signs. If you pick up any of that type of behavior, you have to stay on point and don't let your guards down. You will know what you're up against, and have the option to move forward without enduring the unnecessary consequences of those actions.

Keep in mind; it's consequences to that type of behavior. So don't take it lightly. Always think of how things can turn out if it's not nipped in the bud when it first happens. If somebody feels they can walk over you and have control over you, they will do whatever they want with you. You know what they will say? They will say that you allowed it. This is a true statement.

You also have to watch out for funny characters who want to know how much money you make and want to know all of your financial business. These types of individuals are trained opportunist, they prey on weakness. They usually look for divorced people, married, recently split men/women looking for comfort, and people who appear lonely but have a lot of money.

Opportunists target your pockets, your bank account, and credit cards. Just stay focused, you can be generous, however, don't give away your life savings, or risk losing your investments, your hard working money and your time with a con artist. You might be looking for love, but not in the wrong places. You have to know who you're involved with before you start splurging. There are a whole lot of cases where men/women take advantage. So just use your best judgment of character.

The truth is, the signs are always present in every situation. Watch what's going on around you; look at eye contact and body language. You have to study their behavior.

Main points to remember: Any signs of nagging, selfishness, clinginess, aggressiveness, secretiveness, deception, lack of communication, laziness, aggravation and uncompromising behavior are indications of trouble. All of these actions can lead to problems, unhappiness, separation and broken homes. Therefore, you must know how to counteract these actions.

In a relationship, the key to happiness is communication, friendship and understanding. You must be able to love, forgive, forget mistakes, share and be willing to compromise. If you can't meet the person halfway, things will go downhill, and the relationship will take its course for the worst.

You can't have regrets and you can't hold things bottled up inside. You have to know the true meaning and definition of love, not just saying the words I love you, but actually showing love by every action. People who are together for 50 and 60 years managed to stay together because they understand what love and their connection means. They respect, cherish and devote themselves to their mate.

If you observe long-lasting couples, they had tough times and difficult moments, but they learned how to put the past behind them. They learned how to get past the bumping roads and they remained connected despite the issues they encountered.

No one is perfect. There will be times where you will disagree in a relationship, but when you get aggravated and don't agree with things, you have to learn how keep a certain format... couples need structure.

You must learn how to defuse the tension and remain level-headed, without letting your anger take over. If you don't get mad and furious, things won't escalate into hectic situations. Sometimes it's better to walk away or be silent, then to keep an ongoing battle.

The reason why most relationships suffer is because people are not living the way God designed it. God wants us to learn to forgive. Although we have emotions, we're not intended for our emotions to govern our lives. So many couples have been destroyed because they are doing the opposite of what God intended a relationship to be.

Look at what's happening around you; couples are broken apart, husbands and wives are separated, and children are suffering the effects of a broken home. Where is the love?

Chapter 15

The Power of Love

First Corinthians 13:4 states, Love is patient, love is kind. It is not self-seeking, it is not easily angered; it keeps no record of wrongs. Love does not delight in evil but rejoices with the truth. It always protects, always trusts, always hopes; always perseveres. Love never fails.

Along the way of my journey in life, I had to find out what love is for myself .When I finally experienced the feeling of love there was nothing like it. But some people use the word love so loosely, but they have no concept what love really is. It's not what takes place in the bedroom.

The bible speaks about love and what the word has to say about the matter. And it is very clear that where love is present; there is no room for hate, malice, envy, conceit, anger, lies, or confusion. Love conquers all things and stands in truth.

I believe that the power of love is amazing. Where there is love, there is life. There are no feelings of emptiness and discontent. Where love is present there is no reason to experience hurt and pain. You ever have people who say that they love you but cause nothing but damage in your life? That's not love. Where there is love, there is peace of mind. Where there is love there is no rage or war. Who wants to feel like they're involved with a person who creates nothing but drama and confusion? I know I don't. Where there is love there is forgiveness and no space for revenge. You know I do believe that you have to learn how to forgive. People go through things sometimes in relationships, but you have to learn how to get past all of that and move forward. You can't think of ways to be spiteful as a solution.

I know what love means to me. But what does love mean to you? It's time to examine your heart and mind and think about all the types of love that exist; The love of God, The love of a mother and father has for their child, The type of love that secures long-lasting friendships, The love of a family that sticks together and The intimate love of two lovers.

Now think about what love means to you. How do you define love? Do you know what love is? Some people use the word love, but don't show it. The word is spoken and heard but the action is not seen. Take a look at a battered woman for example. If you do know one, have you ever asked her why she continues to take the abuse before looking in the mirror and watching her self-deteriorate slowly? Once I asked a woman who was in an abusive relationship "He loves me…That's why, I know he loves me." Her response was that he loves her, but that is not love. Love does not destroy. It only builds greater things and evolves as time passes by.

Some many people are blinded because they are continuously searching, they want to feel wanted and accepted. They want to feel like they're loved. So they look for love in all of the wrong places. Every living thing needs love. Where there is the absence of love, there is misery, division and bitterness. The absence of love creates a hostile environment. Why do you think all of these couples are suffering broken relationships? It's because the love has grown cold and is no longer present. Unfortunately, the hostility continues to manifest chaos, and being amongst the unloving, you began to experience coldness in your heart.

It all derives from your upbringing. Some people were never taught to love. They never felt like they were loved in their life. So how could they ever learn how to give love if they don't even know what love is? How can they relate to love when they don't know about all of its attributes in truth? They walk around harboring built up hate for one another. Repaying their new lover back for what their ex-lover did to them years before. It all becomes a cycle repeating itself. I have seen people who walk around with an attitude that has been corrupted and they refuse to learn how to forgive or be understanding. That is because there is no love.

Now let's keep it real. There's something else I want to talk about. What about some family members? Some of us are messed up because of our relatives; still reminded of the facts that some of our own blood forsaken us and left us to suffer. We never forgot. But I have learned that you have to let go of the past. Some people don't know it but let me tell you if you're not aware of this, do you know that your blessing is in your healing? You have to let go in order to move forward. These are facts.

It's not right to hold a grudge inside… that is not love. All of that time and energy you spend trying to get back at someone for something and for what. You make yourself as guilty as them by holding it against them. Yes it was wrong when you faced a tough time in your life and you turned to your family member, but your own blood turned their back on you. It hurts when you think of the end result when you was going through things and a stranger who's not even your own blood helped you out during a difficult situation. Where is the love?

Your own family can sit back and watch you suffer and not even lend you a hand to help you. These are the things that happen when love is not present. When your heart turns cold and you're trying to find a way to get revenge because of a broken heart, that's not love either. I have found out you have to learn to love those who love you and forgive the ones who don't.

If you take a look at the couples of today in the media, how many times have you picked up a magazine and read an article on a famous couple, and read about all of the dramatic details in their life. They're caught out in public fussing, fighting and having shouting matches. Then weeks later you watch a television broadcast and see a news flash that the same couple announced their public breakup. When love diminishes, things like this occur.

When people lose respect for one another and can't communicate without being aggressive and fighting... things start to go downhill. There must be a solution and way to resolve your issues before things escalate to the point where it gets physical.

You don't have to take that route that leads to violence in a relationship. There are ways to prevent a relationship from becoming violent. But you have to learn the keys. The keys are communication, understanding, and forgiveness. You can't hold something against your loved one and harbor hidden malice deep within. You have to learn how to keep peace and love flowing in a relationship.

I have come to the realization through experiences in life that a lot of people are guilty of being unforgiving. They haven't learned how to fully let things go. Instead, they continue to keep an ongoing conflict, whether it's through arguments or hostile gestures. All of that is unhealthy for any relationship and will only cause commotion.

Do you know what love is? True love...You have to learn how to love and I'm not talking about the type of love where you start sleeping around and have different people in your bedroom at night, that's not love.

I'm talking about God. Do you know how God disguises himself? God disguises himself as love. That's right ...God is love. When love and peace is present, there is happiness, joy, and contentment.

In order to incorporate this type of love into your atmosphere, you have to think of ways to keep the love flowing. If you're experiencing a situation and you find it hard to forgive, it's time that you let go. Take it from me, it's not worth it. Do not go on with bitterness bottled up inside. Forgiveness is the key. You have to forgive and let the power of love flow.

Now, I'm not saying if someone is doing wrong by you and constantly violating and mistreating you to let folks walk over you. What I am saying is that you can learn to forgive people for their wrongdoing instead of hating them, fighting all the time and living without peace. Even if they hurt you there is something better out there for you. Just learn how to forgive and move on. Don't let emotions govern your life.

As long as you refuse to let go of the past, it will affect your present. It will determine your every move. At some point you will be left stagnant and stuck in the same position you was trying to get out of.

You have to visualize where you want to be in life and keep moving forward. Forget about where you used to be and what this person did and what that person said. Those are just words. I see too many people get caught up in situations that could have been avoided. If you stop worrying about what people say, you'll be better off. Let it go. Refuse to remain in your old state of mind. You have to renew your mind and change your way of thinking. I am a firm believer in that.

Our thoughts can build us up or break us down mentally. What you think about is very powerful. We have the ability to manifest things through the power of our minds. If you're thinking negative thoughts you will create drama and confusion in your environment. Those things are not of love. Anyplace where there is no peace and no love is not of God.

To know love and understand love you must spread love and allow God's love to flow in your direction. The most powerful love is the love of God because it never ends. It never hurts you and it never ever fails you.

Chapter 16

The Love of God

When God opens the door; no man can close it on you. God is a loving and just God. He saves the lost and heals the sick and feeds the poor and needy. Man will betray you, mother and father may abandon you, but God will never forsake you. The love of God is his mercy; he lets the light shine on the good and the evil doers. God forgives us for our wrongdoings, and corrects our faults.

The evidence of the love of God is all around us. Miracles are happening every day. Doctors tell people they only have a little more time left to live, but yet they're still alive. God helps and loves everyone. Babies stop breathing and are brought back to life and gangsters are reborn again. That's the love of God.

God is love. Love never ends, love never fails you and love never holds an account of wrong. Love forgives, keeps its promises and will not betray you. Now I'm not talking about who cheated on you and who hurt you and all the scandal, that's not love. I'm talking about the love of God.

You have to go through something, to experience what love really is. That is God's greatest gift; love, what God has disguised himself as love. There is a halo over you. The creator of light keeps light shining on you and surrounds you with all the elements required for you to live.

The agape love of God sustains us all. When you walk in God's love, focus on love. I don't mean loving things that shouldn't be loved; don't go to bed with everybody, not that type of love. I'm talking about the genuine love of God.

God is the same God today, as he was yesterday. God's word will never change, only peoples words change. So don't put your trust in mankind, but put your trust in God.

From here and now, until the world comes to an end, God's word is forever. God is the provider of agape love.

Agape love is when nothing is missing, broken, needed or wanted. When you come to that point in life when you do not lack in any areas in your life that is when you have received the agape love of God. Come on now brothers and sisters...give me an "amen". I'm not a preacher; I'm just trying to teach you something... maybe you will listen.

When you reach this level in life, you will see miracles unfold. Doors that were once closed for you will open up for you. You will receive multitudes of blessings and your enemies won't be able to interfere with anything concerning you.

Once God restores things for you, no man and no woman can undo what God has prepared for you.

I've seen people get out of their sick bed. Survivors of cancer, people who were in ICU, breathing through tubes, clinging on to their life almost near the gates of death and they lived to tell the story. God is always in the mix, and his love and grace saves us.

God provides all of our resources and supplies all our needs. I am telling you from learning, experiences. I put all my trust in God. If you let God into your heart and believe in his word, you will live abundantly!

God designed us to live in love and peace, not chaos and confusion, but the sinful nature of mankind rebellious. So God put the law in place for those who rebelled, so they could be corrected and live according to the law.

The problem is that some people have allowed emotions to govern their life, and are living the exact opposite way that God intended. Therefore, there is no order. People are going against the system God structured. In fact, when you go against the arranged order God designed, you are held in bondage. The only way out is to be redeemed and repent of your sins by asking God for forgiveness.

But some people are too stubborn and just want to do things their way and make their own rules. But for how long can you live ungodly and remain unrighteous? Knowledge, wisdom, and understanding are available to all. But some people refused to discover the truth. The fear of not knowing the truth will hold you back. If you want to know the true way you have to search for it.

We all have done things that are unacceptable before God. Everyone has made mistakes at some point in their life because we are not perfect, but we have to make amends for the mistakes we made. Only God can wipe the slate clean and give us a new beginning. You are given another chance to start over and make things right, but you have to be willing to correct your wrongs. If you just keep following the same pattern, then you are just living your life repeating the same cycles over and over again.

God loves us enough to forgive us and have mercy on us. Although man has performed forbidden acts, if you seek redemption, you will see the love of God. God will have mercy on those that seek him and on those who repent and turn away from the things they've done in the past.

When you have the love of God, and you know what Godly love is, you turn away from the old and accept the new. No more lies, anger, hurt, pain, deceit or causing confusion. You learn to walk in God's love and you learn to embrace and display peace, comfort, truth, enlightenment and words of wisdom.

God's love will guide you. You will identify the walk of Godly love, by showing brotherly and sisterly love, by not casting judgments on anyone. Also by expressing forgiveness and displaying love for one another. Without hurting, betraying or belittling anyone. By being affectionate, compassionate, and showing respect and peaceful actions towards each other.

If everything is broken, missing, and you have lack in all areas in your life, you need to surrender to God's love. God's love will shelter you and restore all that are incomplete, separated, and bare.

God is the great protector. You WILL need God's guidance in the world that we live in today. The evidence around us proves that we are living in the last days in time and only God can save us. No one else can save you. Not your sister's and brother's or all of your rich family. Your money can't save you. Your good looks can't save you or the skills you possess. Even all of the smooth talking words won't be able to save you. God wants to change all of the areas that are void. Through my experience, I discovered that once I acknowledged him and put him first then, I then shifted my life into a new atmosphere. When God shifted my life into the next stage where I started to have spiritual growth and became open to change; I knew I was not the SAME MAN.

As I grew in my faith and my spiritual growth, my eyes and my mind were opened to the spiritual man. Every person in this world possesses an inner spiritual being, but you have to tap into it and confess that every living thing is operated by a higher power. Now the things of this world have tried to alter the operation, but God's word stands forever and it will come to pass once the word has spoken on the matter.

In this day and time; people need to open their eyes and see. This is the last days and times where the battle and the fight is not against flesh and blood, but that of the spiritual forces of the system of this world, and only the great redeemer can save us all.

This might be the right time to visit your Christian Church and learn about the word. Start going to a bible study class to get more acquainted with the word of God. Start reading the bible before you go to bed. The idea is to start SOMETHING to walk in the Love of God. You will see how this can alter the outcome of your life for the better!

Chapter 17

The Last Days

This has to be the last days in time. There has never been a time like this with so much increased wickedness, hatred, perversion, wars, hypocrisy, anger, poverty and every form of destruction. If you look at the seasons, you can't even tell the winter from the summer. The weather forecasters can't even predict the climatic changes in accuracy. Love has grown cold. There are mothers against daughters, fathers against sons, and people of the same bloodline who carry deeply rooted hatred for one another. The innocent suffering brutalities, there's bloodshed everywhere, and there are lot of people with malice in their hearts. Matthew 24:12 states, Because of the increase of wickedness, the love of most will grow cold.

If you take a look at what's going on in the world around you, peace is vanishing as the days pass by. There is more hostility and lack of concern for one another. People are lost in their own world, it's like most people are living in a fantasy world instead of reality. But the conscious minded people have opened their eyes and been awakened to what's happening around the world today. Those that are sleeping and not paying attention to the signs, need to snap out of it!

The bible talks about Signs of the End Times, in Matthew 24: 7. It states, Nations will rise against nations, and kingdom against kingdom. There will be famines and earthquakes in various places. If you have paid attention these last few years there have been many earthquakes and natural disasters that have occurred worldwide and have left the death toll high, many people without shelter, food, clothing and a means to survive.

Tsunamis have hit, floods, and hurricanes have destroyed homes, wiped away towns and left behind nothing. The evidence is all around us that the signs of the last day are prominent. The prophecy is fulfilling itself as the generations witness the truth of God's word.

All of these things must happen. The prophecy must be fulfilled. The love of many is tapering off. The heart of men has grown cold. Men have become lovers of themselves. There are many great boasters and people who plot and devise wicked schemes. Women have become flattering with their words more profusely; there is a lot of lust, everywhere that you look, on the television, social media, newspapers, magazines and music videos. Everyone is selling sex. The music has even been influenced by negativity. Many people are filled with conceit and pride. They are arrogant and self-seeking. People are not concerned about the truth. They have made the truth into lies and accept the untruth as what is.

Forbidden and abominable acts and behavior are on display in a seductive fashion as society welcomes what is not a part of God's original intent, structure and design. The world is operating in acts of wickedness; filth, shame and ill regards and have accepted this way of living. They have no morals, values of life or appreciation for what was given to them. The gift of life. Brothers and sisters are bringing destruction and death with them. It is because they don't want change or the chance and opportunity to turn their life around. People are doing anything for money, the root of all evil. YOU KNOW you can't take it with you when you die.

All of the material things are just temporary, but some people don't see it like that and are willing to sell their souls for the fame, fortune and popularity.

Families of today are in deep turmoil. They are suffering the curse of broken homes. There is no love, there is a coldness deep within. There are brothers that hate their own brothers and would kill their own biological brother because the hatred is so deep. As all of these things are occurring; there are great sorrows and tragedies taking place worldwide.

There are countries at wars and battles. Enemies and opponents are battling over the land, the resources of the earth, money, power and the respect; **while innocent women and children are losing their lives**. Every second, another child becomes fatherless because of the corruption in the world today during wartime antics.

There is no unity in the world today. People refuse to come together and unite. Don't you know that we are ALL ONE PEOPLE under God? All that this world consists of is separation, division, and lies. You have the upper class, middle class and the lower. Pretty soon there will be only the rich and the very poor. If you pay attention, you will understand and read between the lies. If you don't pay attention, you will continue to be held in bondage and slavery. Until you decide to free yourself.

There are different types of forms of slavery: mental, emotional, and physical. The mental slavery is the hidden slavery that still exists. People think that they're better than one another or that they're race is the best. If they're lighter and you're darker, they think that they are superior and you are inferior, but people need a rude awakening. In the Day of Judgment, the color of your skin can't save you. Now, there's the gender bracketing where males and females in the workplace are said to have equal opportunities, but the lesser sex gets mistreated and is not treated like an equal at all. Next you have the emotional slavery, the scrutiny of the races. If you come from a race that is looked down upon, where you've always been told that you're nothing and your women are just sex toys, eventually you will start to believe you're nothing.

For example, in certain communities women are treasured, they are in positions of power and treated with respect. Then when you enter other communities, women are treated like objects that are used for the provision of sexual services and are manipulated all across the board. Where their men are calling them out their name and they see nothing wrong with it. Since they have been exposed to negativity, and have been enslaved mentally, they end up having low self-esteem and start accepting being treated like they're nothing.

Then you have the physical slavery, the blood slaves who are the ones who don't know their own identities. They're like clones in a sense. They are taking on the identities they have been programmed to adapt to. They are projected as being dumb, stupid, illiterate and not knowledgeable of anything. So they are treated like the needy and they remain in debt, poverty and bad financial situations. Their minds and bodies have been programmed and they have become part of a system that has them under control. There are many options to explore, but because they have limited their way of thinking, they have not explored every option there is to secure a better situation for themselves. Instead, they are depending on something that is designed to keep them in destitution forever.

We are given mind power and we all possess the ability of awareness. If you want the truth, all you have to do is search for the answers. Signs are all around us, if you choose to ignore what is factual, you are in denial, but your own oblivion can be detrimental.

There is lawlessness all around us. The lawless are prowling around fulfilling their twisted desires and displaying the enactment of sinful nature repeatedly. The word of God has spoken concerning the matters of this world and all of things there are in it. What you reap you will sow, so if you sow a bad seed that's what you will get back in return. But if you sow good seeds, you will have abundance and have a good life.

For those who twist the word, and try to use it for their advantage to hide their corrupted ways, they will be condemned and exposed. The truth can never be hidden or made a lie. What is now will be and what is meant shall come to pass.

Take a look at what's going on around you in the world today. Watch closely and be aware of what is taking place. Choose carefully, make observations wisely, and don't waste time. Whatever you do, do not be afraid, but be mindful of your actions, what must be will be. Your conduct will determine your final path.

One thing to remember, in the last days God can take a fool and turn him into a wise man and take a wise man and turn him into a fool. It's up to you to obtain knowledge. Your conscious is your guide. The truth and wisdom are they keys. Remember, your weaknesses and flaws are the tricks and works of the enemy. So beware because the enemy comes to destroy.

Chapter 18

The Enemy: Comes to Rob, Steal & Destroy

Beware of the enemy. The enemy is always lurking and always waiting for the right opportunity to present itself. He preys on your weaknesses and waits until you least expect it to strike. His job is to rob, steal, and destroy; he leaves behind a trail of misery, unhappiness, and hopelessness.

The enemy is cunning, charming, conniving, convincing and deceptive. He smiles in your face, winks his eye and makes you feel comfortable in his presence, but his intention is to bring you destruction and pain.

The enemy is the father of the lies, the voice of the wicked and the son of temptation and desire. Where there is hatred, chaos, corruption and confusion he is present. Where there is war, jealousy, hate, envy and pride he is waiting. Where there are liars, the unfaithful and the shrewd he lives. The enemy creates darkness, doom, and despair. He is the great manipulator and disguises himself to make people feel secure but he is the great pretender. Through his works, he will keep you in oblivion until you self-destruct.

When the temptations of the world are at hand, the stage is set. The enemy sets the stage because he knows the desires of the heart. Due to man's sinful nature; sin is committed and the seven deadly sins: lust, gluttony, greed, sloth, wrath, envy, pride, all of which lead to the path of destruction.

Proverbs 6: 16-19 states, " There are six things the Lord hates, seven that are detestable to him, haughty eyes, a lying tongue, hands that shed innocent blood, a heart that devises wicked schemes, feet that are quick to run to evil, a false witness who pours out lies and a person who stirs up conflict in the community."

Violence, corruption and innocent blood shed is the work of the enemy. The enemy is the great oppressor and the accuser. He creates confusion, wrath and turmoil.

The enemy can make what is wrong appear to be right and what is correct appear to be incorrect. Many people follow him; they are seduced by his irresistible offers of (lust by sex, greed by money, wrath by drugs, envy by hate tactics and all of his wicked works) unlimited pleasures. But those who follow him and accept his way will perish if they don't repent of their wickedness.

The bible talks about the road that leads to wickedness and many will follow that road. The broad and wide road which is the pathway to eternal damnation. Those who do not repent will suffer the result of not departing from their evil ways.

We have to be reborn again and be redeemed so that all of our wrong doings won't be counted. But if you continue to do the works of the enemy for your entire life and are not saved you will face God's final judgment.

The enemy wants to deceive as many people as possible, look at what's happening around the world today. The innocent are suffering, the youth are killing one another and people are being robbed of their most valuable possessions. The schools are no longer safe; city workers are fighting their attackers, people are taking their own lives, and there is a lot of calamity. **All of those things are the work of the enemy.**

It all starts with your mind. **The mind is your most powerful tool**, but you have to be strong mentally. A lot of things that occur are premeditated; it's the way that people think that determines what kind of life they have. A weak minded person can be easily influence; however, since we all have free will, we know what's right from wrong.

Some people think they can go around causing havoc and terrorizing people all their life. They think they're untouchable and if they get caught, they'll just end up getting locked up and when they get released they'll be back home and go back on the streets. They just continue repeating the same actions regardless of the consequences of the law.

Ignorance haves people's minds all messed up. There's a bigger picture than that. Whatever you do in life is being recorded. God is keeping account of all the things that we do. You may think that nobodies looking and you've escaped, but you're only sewing bad seeds and bearing fruit to death. God is watching and if you don't repent, he will come as the great avenger and his wrath will follow.

What do we do now? Now that we know what the word has to say about the matter, will people continue to ignore instructions? Will people continue to remain ignorant and evade the truth? Or will people become enlightened and accept the truth on the matter.

If you want to be stubborn and be disobedient and deny and demand the word; the soul that will be lost is your own. I don't know about you, but I'm so glad I've been redeemed and accepted the truth.

The system of this world and the rulers are corrupted. There is always a pretty picture painted and you imagine a happy ending, but if you follow the ways and the things of this world, you will come to see the truth. The lie, the deception, the sweet seduction that draws you in with flattery words is all just a plot to lure you in. Once you're in it, you go deeper and you enter into a maze. You think that you're in control and you think that you're invincible. You want to be tough and you think you are the boss, but that is because you are blinded by all of the pleasures of the world. You can't see what is awaiting your destiny if you continue to go down the wrong path.

Do not follow the path or the crowd that will lead you astray. Do not walk with those who do not walk in the light and always follow darkness.

Do not run to the doorsteps of trouble, go the opposite way and don't look back.

Do not think that it is too late for you to change your life. It is not over you can be redeemed!

Do not focus on yesterday. Yesterday will never return and do not worry about tomorrow. Tomorrow will deal with the matters of the world. Look to the righteous...they will never lead you astray. Walk in love and in the peace of God. Remember your purpose and show improvement. The importance is for you to realize who you are...accept others for who they are and walk away from those who try to change who you are.

Remember what the purpose of the enemy is. It's just like crabs in a barrel trying to prevent the one who wants to escape from climbing to the top. If you become a part of the wrong circle, you will become just like the crab that's looking for a way out.

But what do we do now? That is the question for you to decide. What you do with your life and what you do in this life will determine your future. It will deliver you to the path you have chosen. It's up to you to decide. I have told you what path I have chosen, but I cannot make the decision for you. I hope you will look at it like a seed that was given to you that you never want to depart with and make the right choice in the end.

158

Chapter 19
What Do We Do Now?

What do we do now? Now that we are aware of the days and times that we are living in, and now that the signs are all around us. For those of us who are believers, there is one truth.

It's time for a change, but people can't just talk about it, they have to do something about it. People have to break the cycles and create a change in their life.

If you're not living right, then it's time to get right with God. It's time to shift your life into another direction and change your focus. If you're unaware of what's going on around you, then it's time for you to be awakened, and take a look at all of the things that's happening in the world.

Learn to love the unlovely and let go of the grudges. Stop making excuses and putting things off, and stop worrying yourself and stressing yourself out about issues and situations that you are not in control of.

It is time to get focused and no matter what happens, don't be afraid. All of your weaknesses will be tested and used against you. But if you're strong, you will survive and endure whatever trials and tribulations you encounter along the way.

It's time for people to have an understanding of God's plan. It's time to discover your purpose; if you don't already know. If you haven't been redeemed, it's time to be reborn again. I'm not trying to preach to you, but you need to be fully aware because it's time for a change.

Renew your mind and alter your way of thinking. Let go of the hurt, release the pain, remove all of the burdens in your life. Allow your heart to heal. Don't seek revenge, but learn to forgive. Refuse to allow malicious thoughts to surface.

Make peace with the vindictive, by blessing those that don't wish you well. Move forward in life and don't look back, yesterday is gone. You might have failed in the past, but don't let your past blackmail your future.

There is still hope. You still have a chance to have a new beginning in life. You hold the key to your destiny. Your strategy and approach to some of life's most difficult situations will determine everything.

Sometimes you have to stand alone. Don't worry about what your friends, boyfriend, girlfriend, husband, wife, brother or sister will say. It doesn't matter if your aunt, uncle, cousin or whoever is unwilling to support your choice for a change, don't worry. God will place people in your path that will lift you up and take you to where you are meant to be in life.

A lot of times distractions hold people back. The closest ones to you are the ones who will stand in the way of your success, if you don't claim what is already yours. What God has for you is for you. So don't get discouraged when folks try to block you and keep you off track. They can't have the victory. What belongs to you and was originally intended for you is already yours, so claim it.

There are a lot of people that are competitive and envious of what others have, but there's no time to focus on the negative things. Keep your focus on positive things and you will keep positive energy flowing in your direction.

It don't matter if you're a Christian, Catholic, Muslim, Jew, Jehovah's Witness, Baptist, Pentecostal or a Non-Denominational believer; God loves us all. As long as you have a spiritual base and belief system that's all that matters. Staying focused on prayers will keep us stable in the last days and times. People must understand something, you may not agree with another person's belief and doctrines, but don't make a judgments on them.

That is how the division and separation come into play and it is the trick of the enemy, while people are focusing on who's belief system is better, they are losing focus of the main purpose of their life (to be saved) The main concern is to keep praying and continue to believe. Don't worry about what name this culture and that culture uses. Prayer to the divine power is the key.

Don't concern yourself about things of the world, they are just that, worldly affairs. What is meant to be shall come to pass. Avoid passing judgments on one another. Accept yourself for who you are, and let love and light manifest from within. Everything that hinders and harasses you let it go and walk in newness.

It is time to walk in the love of God. Families are separated, brothers and sisters don't speak because they're spirit has grown cold. They refuse to follow God. Families in separation are not exercising the authority given by the divine power.

It's a shame when your own family say, "There is nothing I can do to help you." They don't want anything to do with you unless you got something for them. It hurts when you can't go to your own family when you're in need. It's a form of deeply rooted generation bondage and that suffering is not right to do to your own brother. That's cold. That ain't right.

It's dead wrong, putting lies out and talking about people like a dog. These cycles must be broken and reversed. Love needs to be applied to your way of living. There's too much hateful thinking.

I see it all the time...People are just putting their other brothers and sisters down. But they need to be focusing that negative energy on positive things instead of trying to make somebody else feel bad about their self. People have to get close to world and learn what the word has to say about the matter.

If you read the B.I.B.L.E. (Biblical instructions before leaving earth) We as a people are not supposed to be living like that, not loving and hating one another. If you are not familiar with what the word has to say about the matter...discover what the word has to say. You will then know the truth. Every man and woman has been instructed to live a certain way before they depart from this world.

What we need to do now is to come together and unite. Points to remember, the past is over let it go, forgive and move forward, walk in love, and make peace with your enemies. For you mothers and fathers, even if you're not together; don't let the animosity linger, children need a mother and a father. Do you want your child to know you or know of you? Too many families are suffering from broken homes. For you men that walk out of your child's life that's not cool and you females who leave your kids, you need to be thankful for the blessing of a life. That stuff mess kids up. People count your blessings and remember to be grateful for what you have.

Remember all of the good memories, the times with your family that you can't get back and realize what's important and what is irrelevant that you really don't need in your life. Man I'm thankful for so many things. I remember all the people who had a big influence on my life, like my grandma, she was so nourishing and nurturing. Boy, was she a wise woman, she had so much strength and a strong will power. One time Grandma came back and she had everybody petrified!

Chapter 20
When Grandma came back

Grandma was the rock of the family. She was the one that kept everything together in the family. Her knowledge and her wisdom provided guidance to me and my siblings. Growing up, Grandma played a major role in my life. I trusted her judgment concerning all aspects of my life. Grandma was a praying woman; she believed in the higher power. This helped the family to remain on solid ground even when they were unstable.

Grandma taught me many things and opened my eyes to see the ways of the world and at a young age I understood where she was coming from. She wanted me to have an understanding as a young man. She prepared me for what I was up against in the world.

Grandma knew God and she knew the importance of having a spiritual base. Being saved was a very important factor. Everyone tries not to listen to the Elders, but if you listen closely, they will teach you many things about life.

There are certain things that your elders have experienced and encountered in life that they can prepare you for. Ignorance and an unwillingness to learn is why some people refuse to listen. But sometimes you must compromise and take time to know what is being spoken. Analyze why the words are being given to you as food for thought.

It could be possible that the person is trying to spare you from going in the wrong direction and save you from getting caught up in a hectic situation. You may not see it as them helping you and trying to prevent you from going down the wrong path but in the long run a wise man leads through the enlightening of the mind. What you don't see that is right before your eyes they have already prepared you for. Just listen and take notes for future experiences.

Sometimes you don't have to go through drastic measures or wait to experience reckless circumstances. At some point you have to open your eyes and learn how to view things from a different perspective.

Grandma was the type of woman you could talk to about anything, she was non-judgmental. She spoke her mind and let you know where she was coming from. You couldn't pull a fast one on Grandma, that woman was always on point. She could see through people, she knew who was sincere and who was just plain old phony. That's the discernment of spirit, you can't fool a person who no longer walks and operates in things of the flesh.

When Grandma passed away, her funeral was not your ordinary funeral. I know you're probably wondering what I mean by that, so let me elaborate on it for you.

When Grandma passed away, all of the family, friends, and people close to the family were gathered together. We started reminiscing on old times and talking about the good times when we use to be in the presence of Grandma. Old memories were lingering, as everyone spoke on special moments to remember when Grandma was alive. There were a few tears as we recalled all the good memories we shared with her and those special and memorable moments that you can never get back.

We had a few laughs and everybody continued to share their special thoughts about Grandma. We were talking about times when Grandma had to regulate and times when Grandma showed her love and support for all of us. Then, out of nowhere, we were all interrupted when we heard a loud noise that sounded like something exploded! It was a loud popping noise that sounded like gunshots had went off! **Everybody** ducked and took cover! Everybody was wondering what was going on. I didn't know what to think. Then we looked up and Grandma's casket had popped open and she had risen up out of her casket!! WOW...WHAT?! Now you want to talk about people getting out of dodge and not looking back! I'm talking about people were running in middle of streets almost getting hit by cars just to get away! Drivers were honking their horns and yelling. "Get out the way! Watch where you going!" But people weren't trying to hear all that.

Especially when you think you're going to a funeral to pay your respects and see that person for the last time. Then, all of a sudden, out of nowhere, you think somebody's come to shoot up the place! Like out of a scene of a movie!

It was crazy...how one minute we all reminiscing about old memories and catching up with all the relatives we didn't see in a while and then all of a sudden out of nowhere everybody just takes off like a thief in the night.

It even had me ready to take off for a second...I was like, "Don't tell me somebody trying to run up on us at the funeral? I thought I had to duck for cover."

I guess Grandma was sending us a message; we talked about that for years. It was something that we couldn't forget. Talk about the element of surprise man and that's one thing I can say about black people; if something goes down, a black person is going to get out of sight and ask questions last. Man, a black man will take off like a track runner at the terminator speed if it means saving his life!

Black people are not going to ask what is that? Who's there? All you'll see is their footprints and a trail that led to their escape route!!

The family was wondering what happened and to see grandma rise up like that. I think she was trying to tell us something. I think she was trying to tell us that we all need to come together and live in unity and get our lives together because once you leave you can't come back.

The Mortician said that occurred because of the embalming fluid. They said Grandma had a reaction to it? But man, people wasn't trying to hear that, all they knew it's that they saw Grandma come back and they were terrified!

Can you imagine the facial expression on the kids that was there? I know they had nightmares after that....

Grandma was a very wise woman, and I'm very grateful to have had the influence of a strong woman such as herself as my grandparent. I was truly blessed.

It's very important to have strong influences in your life when you're growing up so that you will see living examples of what strength really is. I'm not talking about the physical. I'm talking about mentally, spiritually and emotionally is what I am referring to. You can have all the physical strength in the world, but if you're weak in your mind you will not survive the world that we live in.

I still remember that to this day. Grandma kept me focused, even when I was growing up, and discovering who I was in life. I never strayed away from her teachings; I always kept her words close to heart. Her words were always with me. Even though I was growing up in a world manipulated by sex, money and drugs that never prevented me from holding her powerful words of wisdom close to heart.

Grandma's love was always present. All that she imparted in me sustained me, even though I explored the world of an American Gangster.

Chapter 21

My views on the American Gangster

Notorious gangsters make an early reputation for themselves and the message is very clear. They're not anybody you want to cross or you'll face the consequences!

Growing up, I was fascinated by gangsters. In my opinion, I believe most people are captivated by people like Al Capone, The Godfather and all the other idol figures of the world. They had money, power, and respect. That's what every man wants in life, but people do unthinkable things for money.

The Power of Money and what money can do is amazing. People look at you differently when you have status and clout. You can take over any territory and make it your domain. In the world of a gangster, money is made, lives are lost and people are made examples of. If you drop a dime, they'll hunt you down till they find you and silence you permanently. This is a world where snitches end up missing. When money deals go bad, the big guns come out and another brother or sister loses their life. It's do or die and you have to have the heart and guts to stomach gangster living.

Once you're initiated in, you're family. There's no way out. If you're disloyal and show dishonor by double crossing anyone that's a part of the affiliation, the henchmen will come looking for you. Interrogation is the torture of a soul. In general, the Henchmen take their victims to a secret location where nobody can hear them scream. The hollers and the deep anguish of a man crying out echoes, but he can't be heard. At that moment, his life flashes before his eyes, but this is the path he chose.

There's a silent code in the streets, so people know what words not to speak. Eyes are always watching, whether it's the DT's or the Feds, informants and witnesses. There's shoot outs and turf wars that are ongoing, until things escalate and it ends up in bloodshed. Finally, somebody becomes top dog and takes over.

To be a gangster, you have to know what it's like to be tough, heartless and emotionless. All it takes is just one phone call and somebody can send a bull dozer through a front window and make it look like an accident, with no trace of evidence.

The world of a gangster is so unforgiving and so cold you might have to take out your right hand man and shed a tear. Things keep going in motion and you'll have to adapt to your environment or get treated like the black sheep out of the bunch.

By the grace of God, some people are spared and given the chance to be redeemed. Receiving the opportunity to change their lives and walk away from gangster living. They are fortunate enough to be saved and leave behind those that travel to the broad and wide path that leads to the demise of our brother and sisters. The road that leads to destruction is shallow, but the road that leads to life you must search to find.

Gangster life is addictive, but I had to turn my life around. I know what it's like to be a gangster, I was in that world, but I'm not of it. I knew I wasn't living right. When your mind is corrupted and you put stumbling stones in your community, you're slowing killing your brothers and sisters. They're dying and you become just like an accomplice.

In the mind set of drug dealers, gangsters and goons, they'll do whatever for the love of money. You can have all the riches in the world, but if you're not right with God and you keep living in sin, you will bear fruit to death. So you have to repent and never return to what you've done.

But if you're in a gang and you don't want to be in the gang anymore, there is a way out. You don't have to be a part of that life anymore if you don't want to. Why would you even get involved in something where you think there's no way out; and if you do decide to leave you have to endure a brutal beating and fight a whole bunch a people at one time just to leave? If you don't want to be a gang member anymore; just leave, disappear and don't come back. Go with a relative from out of town or find a way to start a new life. You don't have to live that way, it's only by choice. You can clean up the slate and change your life like I did if you decide.

When you repent your slate is wiped clean, it doesn't matter what you've done in the past. I made a choice to get out of that life. If you don't repent you're bound to it and you stay in captivity. I didn't want that life anymore. I knew it was nothing but trouble.

So it was a world I had to depart from and once I left my old lifestyle, I couldn't look back. I couldn't allow distractions to draw me back into my old circle. I was officially finished being who I used to be. I cleaned up my act and continued to walk on my new path with a clear conscious.

I actually could say my mind was at ease and I felt an inner peace within. Knowing that I had totally changed and was getting back to a normal, respectful life, there was still a difficult transition, but I got through it.

At first, people couldn't believe that I changed my life around! They were stunned that I did a complete 360 turnaround. They didn't understand that when God has ordained your walk in life, a change is going to come at the appointed time that God has set. Regardless of what people said and what people thought, my time had come to be with God and not of the World. It was my time and I was obedient.

It was all about the timing. God knew his original plan for me and my purpose. My change was meant to be, even though I was out there in those streets and living that life that your momma and your folks warn you about. You know, those boys that your family tells you to stay away from because they're no good, but yet you still end up becoming associated with them.

At that time, I wasn't focused on changing my habits because I was so used to living that way. But then in time, things changed. As the seasons passed by and I took a look at the path I was headed down, I redirected my life to Christ and started to keep my focus on God and helping people by sharing with them my experience and how I came out with the victory despite my past and the treacherous world I was a part of.

The timing was right when I gave up all of those things that were of the World. Now in this day and time, I don't look in the same direction that I use to for comfort. This time around, I can see clearer and I view things from a different perspective and I thank God for giving me the time and chance to be born again.

Chapter 22
Time

In life everything has to do with time. There is an appointed time to be born into the world and a given time where you must die. Everything concerning time is already ordered by the divine power.

No man knows the day or the hour that their eyes will shut closed permanently. No one can predict when their last breath will be taken away. That's why people need to realize the importance of time and what you do with whatever time that you have. As long as you're living and breathing, be thankful for the time that you have each day. You need to remember the importance of time because you can't get back lost time.

Whatever you do with your time determines your future. Your every move is based on time. So spend it wisely, and cherish every second that you breathe. Don't take anything for granted and make the best of your time. Avoid the things that burn your energy. I'm talking about fussing, fighting, drama and all of the unnecessary things that use up your time.

Don't waste your time with foolish people or people who don't want anything out of life. There are too many people out there procrastinating and sitting around doing nothing. Then they tell the same story like a broken record as they fantasize and talk about what they should have done instead of making it happen by taking an action. It starts with a plan. If you want something in life, you have to have a strategy. Stalling will get you nowhere!

Sometimes you can get caught up with the wrong people. If there's something that you need to do at a specific time, those distractions can block you. That can also be the reason why you miss out on what was meant for you at the appointed time.

People have to learn how to stop letting folks just get up in the mix of their flow. If there are things that you have to do, you can't let anything get in the way of that. Another thing that people do that they shouldn't do is spill the beans on every aspect of what they're doing. Unfortunately, that's where they make their biggest mistake. Sometimes people just talk too much. They run their mouth and start talking about an opportunity coming up and then by the time they get their chance to have whatever it is, it's gone and lost because they told the wrong folks. They went running their mouth to folks who really **weren't** happy for them.

There are people in this world who are burning with envy. Really. They don't want to see the next person looking too happy or talking about something that they don't have in their life. Sometimes people will try to draw from your positive energy like bloodsuckers or they'll attach themselves to you like leaches and pour out all of their woes and problems on you. Realistically, you can't take on everybody's problems. There are times when you will have to avoid those people who are always throwing their burdens on you. All of that excess baggage and luggage will wear you down.

The significance of time delivers a powerful message. In our very existence everything we do coincides with time. Our memories that we have all trace backwards to a point in time. Each stage, every season and each cycle all translates into time. No matter where we are or what we're doing, it's all a matter concerning time. Keep time on YOUR side.

So now, that's why you have to come to a realization of doing things with a purpose during whatever time you have in this life. The way you operate every waking day does matter. If you think it doesn't matter or you don't care, you need to do an evaluation of your surroundings and visualize where you think you will end up if you stay in that same place and remain in that same state of mind. If the outcome you picture is unfavorable, then you will know it's time for a change. If you're still practicing your old habits and keep acting careless that's your choice. When reality hits you, once the time has passed and you can't make up for the lost time, you will have a rude awakening. I'm just stating facts.

At some point, our subconscious minds remind us of the things that are close to us and the hidden emotions on the matter. Those are the times when you might think to yourself about something you should have done differently but didn't. Once the time has passed, it's too late to turn back. Thankfully, you can move forward and start out by seeing how you can be a blessing to another life. People need to learn how to give freely without having expectations of getting something back in return. Another thing, people need to stop having regrets. No one is perfect. We all have made mistakes and done some things that some of us may not be proud of. However, if you lost time and want to make up for something that you always wanted to do, it's not too late. You can do anything that you put your mind to doing. If you want to do something in particular, go for it. You can make it happen if you believe. Keep trying until you succeed.

Remember yesterday is gone, so learn to let go of the past. Until you learn to release what hinders you, it will haunt your mind. Don't allow negative things to linger in your mind.

Too many people are afraid to let go of the past. They're still holding on to what use to be. Once that time has passed, it's over and done with, you can't get it back. You have to take that statement into consideration and take the necessary steps to correct your situation in order to move forward. Take your time and do it right!

People are reminiscing about things they need to release and they need to just leave it in the past so they can move forward. Remember, while you live in the past, time keeps going. Time doesn't operate the way people do. Time is always flowing and if you miss your opportunity at a certain time, that's it. So the word is, **"Forget your past to ensure your future."**

That's why people have to learn to be on time (if you're always late, last or out of flow) punctuality is everything. I'm not just talking about showing up at a job, a date or at a friend's house. I'm talking about being on time with the appointed time. People who sit around stalling and sleeping have nothing to do. If you're late or not flowing the way you should, you may miss out on an opportunity that you will never get again or it might take years before the time comes for you to get what you were meant to have years before.

In life, there's a certain time for everything. A time to laugh, a time to cry, a time for new beginnings and a time for endings and to say goodbye.

Some departures are permanent, others are temporary but in life you don't know where friendships, relationships, and close encounters will end up. That's why it's important to appreciate the time you share with the ones closest to you.

A lot of people are living with guilt on their conscious years later. It's because of people they treated badly and used for whatever they could get. When they finally realize how messed up they were and start regretting how bad they treated the person, it's too late because the same one they dogged out ends up dying without ever getting that apology for all the hurt and pain that the person caused them. Then, for the rest of their lives, guilt and remorse stay heavy on their shoulders. Again, **"Don't be THAT person...Be the person that people LOVE"**.

Once time passes by, that's it. You need to put forth a plan so that you don't put off stuff for another day. As the old saying goes "Tomorrow is not promised to anyone". Too many people do that and they shouldn't. Talking about they'll do it next time or some other day. Reality check. You don't know what the next day will bring. Learn to deal with the moment you're in, the here and now. In time, you'll get to everything else later, but don't jump the gun.

Too many individuals in the world today are spending their time getting caught up into drama. Sometimes it's not even THEIR drama! Getting involved in things they have no business being connected to and those things can deter you from making it to the next level in life. Drama, distractions and the people who create confusion cause damage. This can mess people's lives up. That's time spent where you could have been working towards becoming successful in life. Starting your own business, learning a new trade, educating yourself or getting better established while setting goals in life instead of entertaining nonsense.

If you want to get ahead in life, stay away from the drama. There are people in the world who love drama, but you don't have to be a part of it. Make a plan, set a goal and stick to it!

Chapter 23

Drama

Some people think of drama as theatre and a fictional performance with different characters. But, there's real life drama that takes place every day. Let's talk about drama... there's too much of it in the world, period.

Drama is the restrictions on our brothers and sisters today. If you take a look, there's drama present in the media, the exploitation of people and all of the stereotypes. The black woman is being exploited and always being presented as a sex object. If you look at the black man, most of them are calling their women out of their names. To make it worse, these women are accepting this behavior. It descends all the way back from slavery. Think about the mentality of the youth and some of the adults of today. Where is their focus? Acting like a fool just to be seen. Now THAT'S drama.

Look at the court systems. There are too many cases of child support and baby momma and baby daddy drama. There are women fighting over men that don't even want them. The men are losing their lives because they got involved with the wrong women. If somebody wants to cheat and lie, it's not worth fighting for. Why deal with the lies and all the aggravation? The overdrawn apologies and lines about how it won't happen again. Then years later, you're still going through the same baloney. You need to move on with your life. When you want better, you have to leave the losers behind. You must believe that someone BETTER will have the opportunity to come into your life and love you the way you should be loved.

There are people out here with too much insecurity issues. They can't accept their own identity so they pretend to be something that they're not. That's drama. You have to accept yourself and all of your flaws. You have to learn to love yourself for who you are, and if a person can't accept you as is, think of it as their loss. Stop wanting to be accepted by everyone. There may be some folks that just don't like you, but who cares. Focus on what is important; self-acceptance, embrace who you are and love **YOU!**

Don't worry or concern yourself with what people think of you. There are people in the world with real issues. Think about people who don't have a place to lay their head at night and their own brothers and sisters refuse to help them. They can't even reach out to their own family when they're in need. Then strangers end up doing more for them than their own family. How could you treat your own brother like a stranger? Now that's drama.

Think about the young mothers that don't have any money to buy food to feed their children or clothe them. In a bad situation, they're just trying to manage the best way they can and its hard on them especially the ones who have no income to support their families and keep a roof over their head. Placed in a position of poverty, these young mothers are forced to get on welfare just to get by. In addition, these mothers are placed in different government programs to find work. The downfall is most of the jobs that they're referred to offer minimum wages and low salaries, which is not enough to support a household. This now keeps these young mothers in the same poverty bracket. Then they start applying for low income housing because their current rent is too high to afford and they have to keep depending on government assistance. This becomes a vicious cycle. A Merry Go Round if you will. The problem is getting OFF it.

The cost of living is high. The jobs are scarce. In addition, other people, like senior citizens, are struggling and can barely make it off of their SSI checks and pensions. Rent, fees, and fares are escalating sky high and people don't have enough income to make ends meet. Family, friends, and couples are shacking up and doing the roommate things so they won't be out cold in the streets. Talk about drama.

You don't know what drama is unless you've experienced hunger pains. A mom doesn't have money to eat. Your baby needs a new pair of shoes or you don't have the money to clothe your child. In your critical stage, when all you have to your name is the clothes you have on, you're now dreaming and hoping that somebody lets you sleep on their sofa for the night. Talk about drama again.

Drama is when you're living from house to house. You're sleeping at your friend's house, on their sofa, chair, or floor. IMAGINE? You're sleeping on the chilly damp floor with no blanket to keep you warm and you got to go by their rules or get put out in the streets in the blistering cold or snow storm. Experiencing this, you're now trying to figure out a way to get back on your feet.

When you're in a volatile relationship and you have to sleep with one eye open because you don't know if your man/woman might attack you in your sleep, that's the worst type of situation to be in. If you got bruises, scratches, scars and wounds from fighting a crazy and psychotic lover, that's the **ULTIMATE** drama.

There are many forms of drama in life. Drama is worldwide and it can take its toll on you. Drama can wear you down and have you looking all haggard with bags under your eyes. Drama can make you feel like you've been beat down and leave you depressed. Some drama is inescapable, but a lot of drama can be avoided. Sometimes people create unnecessary drama in their lives.

As a word to the wise, if you know you have people in your life who like to create drama and confusion, you need to do the process of elimination. Avoid letting that flow enter your life and rub off on you. That's excess baggage and who needs it!

There are things you will have to turn loose from. Instead of allowing yourself to become all worn-down, you can make the necessary changes to your environment to maintain a comfortable and peaceful atmosphere, as long as you remain in control.

Drama is like the court system, there are a lot of rugged twists and turns and if you're not cautious of your movement you'll find yourself in a predicament you don't want to be in.

Chapter 24

The Court System

Let's talk about the court system. This system can do internal damage to the brothers and sisters of today. Depending on the severity of the situation, but either way you look at it, it's like a conspiracy. You can be found guilty at any point, possibly for a crime you didn't even commit!

There are many cases where people were sentenced and served jail time although they were innocent. Things like this occur when case workers are incompetent and are not willing to do the paper work correctly. The investigators don't do all of the work required to reveal the truth. It's horrible man. These are people's lives and freedom at stake.

When a man has the power to incarcerate you and you have to depend on a lawyer to come to your defense, you're screwed! It's their word against yours and even if you're not at fault, you could end up being falsely accused. Some of these attorneys and defense lawyers are playing on both teams. So, I say, brothers and sisters of today...WATCH your steps!

God is the final judge. Men in high positions with high authority cast judgments, but they are not the finishing author of your life. That's why it's imperative to watch the way you conduct yourselves, because the system is not for no man.

You're already labeled from birth if you're black or Hispanic and there's always a stereotype. Why do you fit the description because of your ethnic background? It's simple, think about slavery and the slave mentality. You will find the answer there.

Does slavery still exist today? When was slavery abolished? People of today need to open their eyes and see what's really going on. It's a mental thing. The idea of being superior or inferior, which one are you labeled as? At the end of the day, somebody has to be at the bottom of the barrel. Who will come out on top?

At any given time, you can be made an example of if you're not careful. You can just be driving down the street on your way home and get

175

pulled over and face interrogation. Meanwhile, while you're out getting questioned and harassed, there's somebody out there with a real situation that needs help. Damn, real crooks are escaping doing Felonies and regular folks are getting harassed!

You got cases like dirty landlords, and domestic cases that could put people behind bars. You might have to plead guilty even if you're innocence or end up facing more jail time. How crazy is that?

Then you have the option of community service and that's "IF" the judge sees fit to give it to you. Now, let's touch on this topic. If you get community service, you have to be subjected to being treated like property of the state and do hard labor like a slave.

Then there's the child support system. Men and women of today need to get it together. If you got kids together, you need to come to a financial agreement to support those kids, even if you're not in a relationship anymore.

Do you want the man all up in your business? The man shouldn't have to be placed in the position of authority to order you how much to pay for a child that you brought into this world. It's too much of these cases going on. If you bring a kid into the world, PLEASE take care of it.

Incarceration is not a joke. Confinement is a restriction of the mind, body and soul. You can't go home and are told when to do everything each day you wake up. It's like a nightmare. Only you "can't" escape because it's reality.

Brothers and sisters of today, get your mind right. Where is your focus? If you're not living right, it's time for you to get your life in order. Don't wait, just do it now. No matter what the case is, you can have a second chance to get back on track and fix the things in your life that you can make better.

Realize that time keeps on ticking. Whatever you do with your time will determine your future. If you get caught up with the wrong crowd, and get locked up, that's lost time. You can't get that time back. That's time you could have used to push your dreams and obtain the things you want in life.

The court system is not designed or structured to benefit you if you're living reckless. So don't expect any sympathy party. Sometimes people can be in the wrong place at the wrong time as well. They end up being guilty by association, but overall just watch your movement. Remember somebody is always watching.

If you make the wrong moves in life it could really mess you up. There are so many people who are stressed on a daily basis and suffer from depression. What about all of the other things that comes about when you got too much on your plate. If you start thinking about all of the things gone wrong in your life, you will stay down and continue to feel overwhelmed and hopeless. Eventually, you'll start to feel alone and powerless if you keep your focus on things that you shouldn't allow governing your life. Until you just feel lost like you have no place to go, no one to turn to. You are trying to face the world on your own with no place to turn like a person struggling, facing troubles and woes. It's like experiencing the raw feeling of homelessness. Being homeless is no joke; it's an awful feeling when you don't have a stable place to lay your head at night.

Friends and family are not always there during the touch times. Sometimes you have to stick it out and face those tough battles where the ones closest to you can't be there for you. It can get rough out there in the streets. When you're all alone and feeling like there are limited options, always remember there is a solution. Just when you think that it's over and there's no way out, there is a way and you will get through the toughest battles if you only believe. Don't be fooled into thinking that it's over. The obstacles that you face in life are temporary. Even if you feel like nothing's going right, hold on and be strong and things will get better. You could be out on the cold streets and face homelessness, but that's not the end of the road. It starts with you. If you believe that your situation will be improved and you stay focused, everything will fall back into place. You have to have faith... and KEEP the faith.

Chapter 25

Homelessness

I had lots of ups, downs and falls. There were many times with unpredictable weather. I didn't know what was headed my way, but when I got hit, I got hit hard. I was totally unbalanced and when I fell down, it felt like I couldn't ever get back up. However, I got back up as many times as I fell, only to rise again and stand as a stronger man.

As I stated in an earlier chapter, tomorrow is not promised to no man. Each day is a gift. Every experience is for learning and life is a blessing. Nothing should be taken for granted. Every smiling face might not be a hello and every good-bye may not be an ending.

In life, you never know when you'll hit rock bottom. You never know what hand you'll be dealt, and even if you have it all, you don't know if you'll know what it feels like to be without one day.

Although, growing up I lived a comfortable life. I didn't know the feeling of being without. When you have a roof over your head, money in your pocket, and you grow up in a neighborhood where you are surrounded by wealth, you don't think about not having.

I was accustomed to always having, but then the harsh reality of how the tables can turn in life hit me in the blink of an eye. That same homeless man that you see on the street every day. The person with no money and no food to support themselves; it can happen to anyone.

When I experienced what it felt like to be homeless, it felt horrible. It was not a good experience. Homelessness is a choice. I made the wrong choice.

Anyone can fall. We all make mistakes and experience difficult situations at some point in life. Don't make things more complicated for yourself if you find yourself facing hardships. What matters are the decisions and choices that you make. It's all about what you do when you get back on track and finally end up back on your feet. In order to keep afloat, you have to have that type of mentality where you see yourself making it no matter how bad things are looking for you. Staying down is a choice. You can rise back up and have more than you had when you fell, "IF" you make the effort.

Take the initiative to get help and support for yourself. There are many options for a person facing homelessness. You don't have to ride the trains up and down or be harassed by thugs. DON'T sleep from house to house, parks or in staircases at night. It's all about choices. Ultimately, you need to make the best choice to better your living conditions.

There are shelters, homelessness prevention programs and alternatives. If you're on drugs, you can go to the hospitals which refer you to a detox program. There are half way houses, three quarter houses or places where you can go to get help and get off the drugs. They have places like the Bowery Mission, for men that will provide shelter until you get back on your feet.

Remember, as long as you refuse to get help your situation will remain the same. But, if you explore some of the available options it will prevent you from remaining homeless. It's pretty simple.

People will kick you when you're already down. Your own family will turn their back on you, and it hurts. So, when you are facing a difficult time in life, always remember you are not alone. There is somebody out there in life going through a worst situation then you. You might find yourself in a bad predicament, but there is always help available. Guys, it's up to you if you want to utilize it.

As long as you look ahead and take the steps to get out of whatever you're going through, you will make it. Tell yourself that you're going to make it. Believe it. When I went through some things that seemed like it wouldn't get better, I kept the faith. I believed in the power of God. Even though some things appeared to be unfixable, God took care of it. I couldn't depend solely on my own abilities. I had to give my burdens to a higher power. Just think of the points to remember. There are alternative options to being homeless. Help is available. There are places that will help keep you off the streets and provide shelter, clothing, and food. There are organizations, churches, and food pantries. If you're facing a tough time in your life, don't give up. You will get back on your feet.

When I was homeless, it was all because I made a choice to live that way. I was living for the moment and at that time I wasn't taking advantage of the options available to me.

I'm sharing with you and being candid about the route I took so that you will learn from it. Being homeless was unpredictable, dangerous, impulsive, dirty, and time consuming (trying to find food, drink and a place to sleep each night). It makes you vulnerable in certain situations. From one minute to the next you don't know what's happening. People take advantage of you this way.

Facing all of those cold nights was not easy and riding up and down on the train was no way to live. It seemed like I wouldn't be able to recover from all the damage being homeless caused. I mean, it messes with you mentally. How? When you know you don't even have a place to lay your head at night, and you can't even use the bathroom when you want to. The things that people take for granted are the things that you wish for when you have no place to lay your head at night. Sometimes I wished for a comfortable bed, a warm shower, and a good home cooked meal. So, not being able to have those things made me only imagine what it would be like to have a regular life and job again. That way of living continued until I did something about it. I started to devise a plan.

I am living proof that you can turn your life around. No matter what anyone says about you. They can call you whatever they choose to, but you have the power to make a change. I knew at that time that I couldn't continue to live that way. There is a strong force inside of me that said it's not over. The battle that I was fighting was temporary and by the grace of God, I came out with the victory! Now, I will continue to fulfill my purpose. I'm not looking back. Yesterday is gone, but today I walk by faith and not by sight.

I'm so thankful to be saved by grace. I hope that the insights I share will help someone. If I didn't listen to that inner voice, I could have still been stuck in the same position. It's so important to listen. The outcome of where I am today could have been different if I refused to listen.

Chapter 26
How important it is to listen

The bible talks about a wise man will increase in learning, but a fool despises it. You can never correct a scoffer. Why? Think about what a scoffer does, they will keep leaving scuff marks wherever they go. They will remain a scorner.

Listening to instructions is extremely important in life. The laws, rules and teachings are given to us so that we can have structure in our lives, and be in the position to build a foundation. Some people don't want to hear all of that talk from my point of view. I believe that some people are ignorant in some ways and refuse to follow order. You can't always act like you're pig headed all your life. God gave us instructions for a purpose. There is a certain way we are supposed to carry ourselves. We can be builders in life and grow up to become strong men and women who will lead the next generation for the hopes of a better tomorrow. You need to not lead one another into destruction and ruin everything that is meant to be cherished and sacred.

When people are disobedient and do not listen to instructions, there are consequences that follow for not listening. That's why you must learn to listen.

There is so much sin in the world, which is the result of people despising instructions and thinking that they're living the way they choose to. But, it's not that simple as they think because every man has to give an account and answer to God.

It doesn't matter what you think or what you feel. You can believe whatever you want to believe and choose not to listen. Know that there will be a price to be paid for every disobedient individual in the eyes of God. Some people laugh and carry on foolishly, they don't care. But if they keep having that same mentality, one day they will see the outcome of following their own way or following others and not listening to what the word has to say about the matter. There are some things that are so clear to comprehend but some people like to evade the truth. The truth is the truth.

There are times when you will have to depart from that crowd that despises instructions. The ones who like to run around and want to live according to the rules of the world. I'm talking about living in lies, lust, and confusion. Getting high and abusing drugs, sleeping with different partners and taking advantage of people. Destroying the community by terrorizing the weak. All of those things are taken from you. They hold your soul in bondage when you sew to the flesh and the desires of the material things.

I had to learn from insights and all of my experiences. You have to learn how to listen. Most people don't want to listen. They want to talk. When you spend too much time talking and not listening, you can miss a lot of important factors.

Most people who despise instructions walk down the wrong path which leads to destruction. It's not worth taking the risk of the consequences that follow long-term. It's not worth ending up in an institution, penitentiary, or dead in a grave six feet under.

As I said before, smart men don't go to jail. Smart men increase in knowledge and become wise men. It's all about the choices we make. Jail is not a place where you want to be. Forget keeping up with your friends. It's a horrible feeling knowing you gotta be there and can't get out. Your there until a panel says you can leave. It's a trapped feeling. Don't go there.

When I had to do some time it was the worst feeling of being confined. There were so many things I could have been doing on the outside, but I got caught up in the trap. That's why I had to turn my life around. I couldn't continue to follow my way. Now I have my story and my message to share with the generation of today. You don't have to follow the crowd to be accepted. You don't have to impress anyone just be yourself and most importantly don't worry about what people think and learn to listen.

That's why it's important for parents to raise their children and bring them up the right way. Kids need to be guided by leaders. They need to be around the right individuals because what they hear is everything. You know what I always think about? WHO are the people that our kids look up to? WHAT are the kids listening to? What is the effect the powers of words have in their life?

Some kids don't want to listen to their parents or elders in their life. Instead, they choose to listen to their peers. I have learned through my experiences you have to be careful "who" you listen to.

If you listen to the wrong person and follow them, that person could be leading you to your death, biggest downfall in life or the greatest disappointment.

Learn what is required concerning listening. There are many teachings that give examples of what happens when you don't listen. If you keep your focus in the wrong direction, you will be led astray.

In a fool's paradise, he believes whatever he hears. As he sets out for his adventure, the warning signs are all around him but he does not pay attention to reality. Although evidence and caution signs are right before his eyes, clever and cunning people convince the fool to indulge in mischief and he thinks nothing of it, then he comes to a dead end.

Don't be like the fool. Don't get caught up in situations that could've been avoided only if you would have listened. There are a lot of situations I escaped because I thought about what the elders use to tell me and analyzed everything. After I questioned what was given to me as a guide to assist me in maneuvering through some of the obstacles in life, I understood why the elders shared certain accounts of their life story with me. The stories were meant to deter me from choosing to walk in the wrong direction. Those tools are very important and if we use them correctly they will help shape our lives the right way and keep us on the right path. Sometimes you have to learn from the mistakes other people made so that you will be fortunate not to go down the same road. You will walk in the right direction instead of making a wrong turn.

Some people don't want to hear all of that wise talk. It's not important to them so they think. People need to realize, like I understand, your mother, father, grandmother and siblings have shared certain things with you because they were trying to prevent you from going down the wrong path in life. Be thankful if someone takes the time out to help you. In today's society, some people are so cold hearted, ungrateful and inconsiderate.

I could have made worst mistakes if I didn't have the people in my life that guided me and took the time out to contribute to a better cause. Now, I'm sharing my experiences with you and although some people don't want to take heed, the truth still stands.

I'm keeping it real and I'm not sugar coating anything. Some people walk around like nobody can tell them anything and refuse to listen to the truth. Walking around with big egos thinking they know it all, but you don't know nothing if you deny the truth. That's just plain old ignorance. Some people are living a lie and refuse the knowledge that is always available. But lack of knowledge and refusing the truth will get you nowhere in life.

Points to remember. It is important to listen at all times. Evaluate and analyze the words that you hear, decipher why the words have been spoken. A person who cares for you will try to correct you and better you to build you up not break you down. A mother or father will scold you to protect you and teach you right from wrong. A teacher will teach you what they know, but it's up to you if you want to learn. In conclusion: A deceptive person will only mislead you, but a concerned person will guide you.

No one is perfect. We all make mistakes. However, a lot of life's obstacles occurred at some point in our lives all because of not listening. It's imperative that you listen. If you do you will exceed in everything that you do. Also, I feel like people need to watch what they put on display for the world to see. People need to be careful how they project their character.

Chapter 27

The Camera

I want to touch on a topic that needs to be addressed. One of the greatest inventions known to man is the camera. The camera captures your essence; it's seductive and leaves people mesmerized.

Although cameras can capture your best or worst moments, and all of your accomplishments, the camera can also be used for manipulation. The camera can be used for black mail or can jeopardize your life long career if the wrong individuals use it to take your pictures and videos.

Cameras are used for evidence and show proof of what occurred. They tell a story. We use cameras to take pictures, make movies, videos and record and depict events of our life story. There are some things that are better left unsaid. For example, people use the camera to expose things that should not be spoken of.

If you know you were once involved in criminal activity, why would you get on the camera and tell? I was down with so and so and why are you televising it and snitching? It's better to say nothing at all!

There are people profiting and capitalizing off of the come home story and its nonsense. They will pay you to do a "Tell all book". In the meanwhile, you're ratting people out, exposing the innocent and exploiting yourself.

There's nothing wrong with exposure, but if you've got to exploit yourself, that's the wrong type of exposure. Some things should not be disclosed. It's all about making a profit and generating revenue. No one cares if you get negative viewpoints or what happens to you after the camera stops rolling.

It's just like women who expose their sex lives and encounters with different celebrities. They provide explicit graphic details and the media sells it and a profit off it. This is called exploitation. What about the next generation? They will think it's cool or alright to do it in this manner. It's not worth selling your soul for an image.

Many Idol figures of the world get in front of the camera. You see, you better be careful what you say or do. If you don't it can be used against you. Call yourself changing the game, but not to be nobodies sucker. Watch your movements when you're in front of the camera. The wrong person could be watching.

Set good examples for the youth of today. They follow what they see. The youth need good role models. Brothers and sisters of today, you need to stay on point and keep focused.

Don't get in front of the camera and make a fool of yourself. Don't make yourself look bad or associate yourself with negative things.

If you get in front of a camera not acting right; that will be with you for the rest of your life. People will always remember what you did. The camera catches people off guard. So many people are caught in the act unexpectedly, which can ruin your reputation, future opportunities and business endeavors.

It's not worth ruining future opportunities for stupidity. Everybody wants to be seen, but show yourself in a positive life instead of making yourself look like you don't have any sense.

The way you present yourself means everything. Man, sometimes when I see certain individuals in front of the camera, I shake my head when I see them going out like a sellout.

All of these imposters, informers and people posing like something they're not. People just want to feel important, some people would do anything for attention, so they get behind the camera and act a fool.

However, you can be dead and gone but those pictures, films and videos will still exist centuries later, so be careful what image of yourself you leave behind. Generations after you will have access to it, so leave a good image and make a lasting impression.

When I see people getting in front on the camera acting foolish, I think about how bad they make themselves look. How much shame they bring to themselves without even knowing it. If you want fame and notoriety and have to act foolish to get it, that is what you will be remembered for the rest of your life. People will only remember you being a fool. Most people don't talk about all of the good things that a person has done in their life. The majority likes to focus on the negative things that a person has done. So I say, to all of you out there who have gone that route, look in the mirror. Is it really worth the humiliation and shame to sell your soul just for a name? If you call yourself changing the game, then who's the real player if you're the one left looking stupid? Think about that for a while.

I see it happen far too often. But as for me personally, I feel people need to think consciously before they get in front of that camera talking. Be aware somebody's always waiting and scheming. Unfortunately, it can be someone close to you or a stranger. They are waiting and praying for the opportunity for you or someone else to slip and give even an inch of information which they will use for their own advantage. People need to think consciously about what they're saying before they speak. Instead, make your momma proud of you. Some people say stuff that just makes their mommas shake their heads out of disgrace. Make the right choice.

That's one thing I can say, my momma taught me well. What she installed in me is with me to this very day. Presentation is everything. My momma wouldn't let me go around making a fool of myself. Even when I made mistakes and I was wrong about certain things, momma always put me in my place. I knew right conduct from wrong due to the teachings of momma and she wouldn't allow me to misrepresent her or myself. Through my actions, I always thought of momma. I didn't want to bring any shame or embarrassment towards her direction so I was cautious of everything.

Momma was there with me through the most important stages of my life. She watched me grow from an infant, to a toddler, to an adolescent to an adult. She watched me develop with the hopes of providing the best future a mother could ever give a child. All the sacrifices she made for me was so I could achieve the greatest things. The selfless acts that she demonstrated will never be forgotten. The memories of momma are close to my heart and deep within my soul. It seems like just yesterday, I could hear her voice, but now that's she gone all that lingers are the thoughts of the one woman in this life that no else can compare to. Momma...

Chapter 28
When Momma Passed Away

There comes the day that every man dreads and doesn't like to talk about but we all must encounter at some point in life. I was at work. It seemed like just an ordinary day. My boss and co-workers were all following their daily routine. I was lively as usual and telling jokes making everybody fall out their seats. My day started off good, and I didn't expect anything to go wrong. But just when you least expect it, in the blink of an eye, you are overwhelmed by the element of surprise. When it hits you it hits extremely hard and it can leave you traumatized.

I never will forget that day as long as I live and breathe on this earth. It still lingers deep within my soul and it replays that moment over and over again. It was the day that changed my life forever. The day that I was filled with such a void. I thought that I would never recover.

I received a call from my sister when I was at work. As she spoke, my heart began to race faster. It was bad news about Momma and her condition wasn't looking good. My sister told me to get to the hospital as fast as I can. The words coming out of my sister's mouth sounded like slow motion. I felt like screaming and on the inside I felt like I was being torn apart, slowly.

As my sister continued to relay the news about Momma, I cried deep within. I nearly broke down at my job. The look of hurt was written all over my face. My boss knew it wasn't good news. He said G' take the car and go. I drifted off into a zone far away as I tried my best to gather my thoughts.

Then reality hit me when my sister sent me pictures of momma. When I saw momma, I knew how the severity of the situation. I could feel hurt and pain harboring deep beneath the core.

As I took another look at the pictures of momma, I felt helpless. There was nothing I could do to help her. Then flashbacks started to occur and I couldn't contain it any longer my heart was in distress and it ached tremendously. I just broke down and cried as the tears over flooded like a rainstorm on a cloudy day. I cried all the way from New York to Maryland and I couldn't stop, there was so much anguish. I cried and screamed so much it was to the point where my soul felt like an echo. From Lil G', to Ole G'...everything I am, is because of her. Momma, my sweet and loving momma.

I was all broken down. I knew the end was near, but how could I ever cope? How could you ever say good-by to the one who gave you life? It's hard to let go knowing the departure is forever. It's not like being in another state and knowing that you can always come and visit or it's not like you can make a long distance call and ever hear their voice again. Every man has an appointed time for Momma to depart from this world. You just have to hang in there. Be strong for your family.

I dreaded seeing momma in the condition she was in as I thought about reaching the hospital as fast as I could. I wanted to rush to her aide. I wanted to be there for her like she was always there for me. I wanted to believe that Momma was going to be alright. I didn't want her to leave me, but I didn't want to see her suffering either.

On my way to Maryland, there were so many thoughts racing in my mind that I couldn't keep focused. I knew in my heart this could be the final blow. My appetite had even decreased during my drive to the hospital. Nothing else matter at this point, I just wanted to be there with Momma. I started thinking about Momma's beautiful smile and how I couldn't wait to see her. I wanted to reassure her everything was going to be alright, but I was worrisome that it was not and there was a pounding sensation in my heart as I wondered if this was the end.

When I got to the hospital, Momma was surrounded by my siblings. Love was in the atmosphere. The type of love a child has for a mother. From babies, to young adolescents to adult men and women. We couldn't have made it to this point without Momma. Some parents abort their babies but Momma gave me a chance to live. Momma let me experience life and that is the ultimate gift.

When I looked at Momma, I was so thankful for all that she had ever given to me. As she looked back at me, her eyes were telling me something. At the time I didn't realize it but that would be the last time Momma would ever look into her sons eyes.

Momma had watched me change my life around. I did a complete 360. Nobody would have ever expected that coming from me. Not from someone who was controlled by the street life and the material things of the world. Who would have known that I would be reborn again? Thankfully, Momma got the chance to see me straighten up my act. I gave up everything. The drinking, the drugs and the lifestyle in the past. She fought hard to protect me and deter me from that type of environment. But once I got a taste of the high roller lifestyle, I couldn't escape. I knew all the key players and had access to all the things pleasurable to mankind. I was living without grace. There was no spiritual base, so I kept going in the wrong direction.

However, I was in need of a new beginning. God allowed me to have a new start in life. He took me from where I was and brought me back to where I was meant to be originally. The Great Redeemer set me free. It was through my redemption that I saw a reflection of what uses to be a priority but now those things of the past were all irrelevant. Out of all the things I ever possessed in this life, nothing could buy Momma more time to live. Only the grace and Mercy of GOD could spare her. I witnessed GOD'S miracle works all on that day.

The doctor had administered medication to Momma and it appeared to ease the pain momentarily. Then suddenly, things took a turn for the worst. At first, Momma was watching TV. Things were quite. Then BAM, The next thing I know...out of nowhere, the EEG machine starts going off and making funny sounds which alerts the medical practitioners. I was in oblivion after that. I didn't know what was going on. My sister and brother were outside the room crying. The nurses were running and I heard somebody say, "Call the Priest." I started screaming for help frantically. "Call the doctor! Somebody help! Where's the Doctor?" I said with conviction. But he disappeared. He was like a shadow in the jacket. By the time he reappeared his words started ringing in my ears; "There's nothing more I can do," he said dryly. "What you talking about! Do CPR! Do CPR! I said."

Little did I know the Doctor couldn't perform CPR because Momma did not want to be resuscitated? The band on Mommas arm was an indication that she was a DO NOT RESUSCITATE PATIENT. At that point, I called on the highest name above all names.

I said, "In the name of JESUS, you are not leaving me like that...IN THE NAME OF JESUS Momma, come back...IN THE NAME OF JESUS!" Not on me Momma we got work to do... "IN THE NAME OF JESUS COME BACK!"

Now it may be a shocker to some people, but I watched my Momma come back to life after I called on the name of Jesus. When Momma opened her eyes, I knew it was the miracle works of GOD.

It may be a shocker to some people but I watched my momma come back to life after I called on the name of Jesus she raised from the dead. The doctor didn't have the power or authority to revive her, only the name of Jesus. When Momma opened her eyes, I knew it was the miracle works of God. The nurses and the doctors were astonished. They couldn't believe what they had just witnessed. But yes, Momma was brought back to life through the strong power and faith of the belief in the miracle of God. That if we, as conscious minded people, believe in the works of the divine, being firm believers in the unlimited powers of the manifestation of God, we would experience miraculous works and receive a multitude of blessings. This was sent forth from God to remind all believers that he is omnipotent and that the miracle is in the faith of the believer of the works of God.

My belief and my faith in God is so powerful, that God made the miracle happen. When Momma came back to life; believers and non-believers witnessed divine intervention that only a higher power could reveal to mankind. God can make what seems like it's impossible, possible. All you have to do is believe. If you continue to have faith, you will watch miracles unfold as I did. They will come simultaneously and you will see Gods works. This is my affirmation, you must see the vision and have the expectation of the result as you visualize it as it manifests.

I believe in miracles and when the miracle took place Momma got the chance to rededicate her life to Christ. That was another blessing. She didn't travel to the other side without wiping the slate clean. Do you see Gods plan? I believe that God used me, her son, as the medium to intersect through the act of faith so that she would have the opportunity to be saved and deliver a testimony of the confession of her acknowledgement of her belief in Christ to receive deliverance through the act of repentance.

All that is required is for you to become a believer, to repent and confess your wrong doing and allow God to deliver you from the sinful nature. When I let go of the sinful nature and looked to God concerning every matter, God demonstrated to me that it is imperative to put him first. If you don't you will end up lost amongst the broad and wide road that leads to destruction. I put my trust in God and I put him first in all matters and things started to change when I submitted to his will. I believed in his power and he let Momma live for an extra hour. After that, it was time for her to rest. She took her final breath, and when her eyes closed. My soul cried out, "Momma."

After I left Momma on that hospital bed knowing I'd never see her again in this life, the hurt and pain took its toll. I cried and screamed so much to the point where it felt like there was a piercing sensation deep in my soul. This type a pain was the worst pain I ever felt in my life and for days it just wouldn't go away. At night, I couldn't sleep, I couldn't eat, and I just felt like I couldn't go on another day. There were so many things that I wanted to say that I will never be able to tell her. The thought that I will never be able to hear her voice out of all people in this world drowned me in a bed of tears and sorrows.

So many thoughts raced through my mind. Momma did everything in her will power to keep me and my siblings out of trouble and I am the man that she reared me up to be. I exist because of her. The way she dressed me and kept me looking sharp and impressive at all times. Momma always gave me the best things in life. She introduced me to living abundantly. I recalled how she took me to Martha's Vineyard. She always showed me the finer things in life and encouraged me to obtain it. She taught me not to have any limitations as to what I could accomplish in life. That stuck with me. I will always remember the way she gave me direction when I was distracted by my peers.

Momma gave me so much. I am so appreciative to be born of a woman who gave her heart and soul, to give me the nothing but the best in life. I'm grateful she got the chance to see me have a legitimate job and change my way of living. I became more established and accepted the fact that although we all make many mistake, there's always room for correction. Anyone can straighten up their act. When Momma got to see me walking on a new path, it made a difference. No matter what anybody said, Momma always believed in me and had my back.

She watched me excel to higher levels in the workplace. I advanced from one position to the next, while I accomplished opening up my own business. All that I can achieve, I know I will succeed at. The only thing that I thought of now is that Momma wouldn't be there to give me a good word or a listening ear. She wouldn't be able to see further progress and the great things in life that I will do. I won't ever be able to tell her about my success stories. But I thank God for the influence and the role she played in my life. In my eyes... she was the greatest.

Chapter 29

The Funeral

I had many sleepless nights after Momma passed away. I did a lot of tossing and turning in my bed too. It hit so hard I wanted to believe it was just a terrible dream I awakened from. But the days were winding down, getting closer to the time me and my family had to bury Momma.

When the day arrived to bury Momma, no one could understand the level of the pain deep within, unless they lost one of their parents. The absence of words. Not even the things I delight in could soothe the hurt. The way it affected me mentally. This was the biggest loss I have ever encountered. The loss of a parent. This feeling is incomparable to losing a friend or a relative. If this has happened to you already then you know what I'm talking about.

Mourning for a parent is the type of mourning that lingers deep within your soul. It's a type of hurt and pain I never felt in my life. It just left me completely broken and empty inside. It hurts so badly when you remember all the traditional things you use do together that are passed down from generations. It kills you inside when you realize that the next holiday won't be spent with them. Their absence leaves you in a stoic state. You never forget what it was like having them around; reminiscing and now learning how to cope without them.

Momma's funeral was massive. It was like burying a Queen with Royalty. Everyone I can think of was there to show their respect. There were so many people that the funeral home was overcrowded. Every time I turned around there was someone else expressing their condolences and showing acts of sympathy. I was so overwhelmed. There were moments where I just needed to find someplace quiet to be by myself to meditate and ask God for strength to endure this difficult time. I could feel myself getting weak, but during it all God sustained me and allowed me to humble my spirit. Even at times when people came up to me...and didn't know what to say, they just wanted to say something. Unaware that at a time like this, some things are better left unsaid. I had just lost my Momma; I didn't have any time to entertain nonsense.

After Momma was laid to rest, the aftermath took its toll on me. It was time for all of those people who came out to show their love and respect to the most special woman in my life to go back to their homes whether in NY or other states. We all had to now fact the fact that this special woman would no longer be with us. Tears just kept flowing from my eyes and the pain was so intense. There were days when I couldn't eat for the entire day and my phone would ring non-stop and I just wouldn't answer for nobody. My voicemail was so full that no one else could leave me a message. I just needed the time to grieve. At first, I became restless. That was during the first stage of grieving. There are three stages in grieving. In the weary stage, the first stage of grieving; I disconnected from the rest of the world. I did not want to be reminded by anything or anyone that would make me remember I just lost my Momma. Then in the second stage; the missing stage, old memories kept lingering and I kept reminiscing about the past and how things use to be when Momma was around. I remembered every precious detail about her and how important she was to me. Then in the last stage, the third stage; in the healing stage, I regained my spiritual strength and managed to be receptive to the healing process after losing a loved one.

The healing process did not happen overnight. There's nights I woke up in the middle of the night and cried like a baby...my pillow was soak and the tears kept pouring down like rain. Gradually, I reconnected with people who had been trying to reach me and I found people who couldn't get in contact with me. I found ways to keep myself busy as I focused on my many goals and aspirations. I worked on projecting my ideas. Most of all; I continued to pray to God for more strength.

As I prayed I grew stronger each day. God enabled me to carry on and altered my mind set so that I could continue down this new path God provided for me. I worked towards living according to his will because my will won't be done and Gods will; it will be done. Now all the angels in heaven say amen!

Thank God that I can now walk around not like Clark Kent. I can walk around like Superman and stop acting like a mirror man. Men and women of today need to stop acting like Clark Kent and Wonder woman. Instead of acting like Clark Kent let God put his super on your natural. With God, I was like superman. I was given the ability to do unthinkable things effortlessly. Like hair lye, you have to allow God to put his super on your natural; it's like putting a straightening on nappy hair.

I thank God I have the power to endure to know what it was like when she was here. We were all taken by a loop when it happened. Thank God for helping us not to remember those things as they came to pass. "You know what I mean," as Momma use to say.

As time passed by, I was able to proceed without all of those memories haunting me to the point where I couldn't make it. It's by God's grace that I made it because I had those days where I felt like I just couldn't carry on another day. Then I started to see clearer. My soul was weary, but God helped me to maintain.

I thought to myself..."What's a man to do now?" Now that Momma was gone, I thought about where I stood as I man up against the things of this world. With God by my side, no battle is too great for me. I knew it was time for me to make it or perish...

Chapter 30

Make it or Perish

When Momma passed away I knew I had to make it or perish. The realism of the current state of things stared me right in the face. There was no way for me to escape the harsh reality. This was real and I had to deal with it one way or the other. Thoughts of what took place started resurfacing. I could feel the pit of my stomach turning. The experience of losing her filled me up with feelings of helplessness and despair. I wasn't prepared for the aftermath of the day Momma's eyes closed. She played the most important role in my life and without her my life felt like it was full of emptiness.

I felt like I was lost in the wilderness with no place to turn. It's like I could feel myself deteriorating slowly. I needed to hear Momma's voice. I wanted to taste Momma's cooking and I wished I could see Momma's face once more. I didn't want her to leave me so soon. All the time when she was here, there were things that I wanted to say to her but never got the chance. There was nothing else that mattered to me at this point. I needed the love of a Mother. I felt like that innocent child searching and trying to find substance. Now that Momma was gone I stood all alone in this cold cruel world.

Thinking of the past, I would think back whenever I had feelings of uncertainty about any situations in my life and I would call Momma. I called Momma and told her whatever was on my mind. She understood me. She listened to me and spoke words of wisdom. The world could rise up against me, but Momma would stand up for my defense.

As I drifted off into a zone things became very clear to me. Although I was grieving and I didn't want to say good-bye, I wished there could be a forever. As much as I remembered all the beautiful memories, yesterday was gone and I didn't know why she had to leave so soon. But as much as I loved her, I knew I had to learn how to live without her. That was the hardest thing for me to do since I felt like the light of my world was no longer shining.

I had to get myself together. It seemed like I would mourn forever; my strength was fading but I had to hold on. It was not easy at all. That was the roughest time in my life. I couldn't ever hear certain songs that Momma used to love. It brought back too many memories; I had to turn off the radio.

I felt like I was going to sink and soak in misery. Not having Momma around was detrimental. What kept me grounded is the structure and foundation Momma built. She didn't raise me up to be weak minded. Her guidance and her teachings never departed from my mind. Her instructions were a reminder to me not to depart from order. Therefore, I refused to let go and I waited on my change. If I soaked in misery for the rest of my life and let my spirit die, I would be left to nothingness.

The grace of God restored my strength. God granted me inner peace deep within my soul, and he directed my path. God gave me a reason to hold on. I once was unstable but God put me back on solid ground. The love of God took me out of a place full of desolation, and renewed my mind, body, and soul. I was restored.

Now it was time to focus on my change. I had to reposition myself in life. Turn my energy from negative to positive. Every person and everything I deposited into my life was for a special purpose. On this new path in life, I eliminated everything that I considered toxic and detrimental to my environment. When I entered this new atmosphere my vision was clearer and I confirmed my affirmation that I would not perish. I was determined to make it.

God made me to prosper and live in abundance so that everything I touch should multiply not diminish and be depleted. When a man is lost in the world and refuses to depart from sin and obey the system of divine power, he reaps the seeds of his own confusion. Destruction will come upon him.

It may seem like there is no escape, but the only way out is through redemption. That is the only way you will make it. You must be redeemed and be reborn again so that you will not perish. I have learned this through my mistakes, trials, tribulations and submission to a higher power.

You must submit to the divine power. How long can you live in sin? How long can you live in pain? How long can you go on hurting people? How long can you live your life without substance and direction?

A man who refuses instructions will perish due to ignorance. The man who continues to be arrogant and is not receptive to what he hears will be punished. The man who hides from the truth will be exposed.

In life you have an important decision to make. The road that leads to destruction is broad and wide. Many will follow that road and they will perish. But you shall not perish if you want life. You too can walk in newness like me.

I exist for my purpose. My purpose is to share my story. Teach what I know and lead the way for those who have entered the wrong path. It's not too late to turn around. Like myself and many others, I realized there is a way out. God gave me the opportunity to experience what it's like to walk in newness. He gave me a new beginning.

You can have a new beginning too. It does not matter if you once were a gangster, drug dealer, alcoholic, drug addict, prostitute, con man or robber. Whatever you are, it does not matter. God can wipe the slate clean and give you a new start in life. All you have to do is ask God for forgiveness and accept God into your heart.

If you're ready and willing to make a change today, walk on a straight path and want your life to be redirected to Christ, say this simple prayer for forgiveness: Father God, I now accept your son Jesus Christ into my heart. I believe Jesus Christ is Lord and Savior. I am a sinner forgive me for my sins and I ask you to direct my path in the name of Jesus, Amen.

Hopefully, you will be ready to make the change. However, if you're not, just keep in mind, no man is promised tomorrow. When your eyes are closed permanently, there is no activity in the grave. It is time for people to live conscious minded and realize the consequence is too severe to ignore. As long as you're alive you have the opportunity to be redeemed. Therefore take heed to these words and let the redeemed say so.

You don't have to look to friends, family, or strangers for affirmation. The evidence of the works of God is right before the eyes of all of the Nations. People just have to recognize who their source really is and stop worshiping idol figures of the world. I looked to God and he opened up doors for me, and sent the right people in my direction like a chain reaction.

Chapter 31

The Round Table

It takes key players who are dedicated to their skill to congregate and create a powerful effect in life. All minds come together on a mutual understanding. Every party involved has the same concept. It's like putting the missing pieces together to a puzzle. When they all connect they become one body. This is the "Round table".

When it's time to go to war and the enemies end up defeated, it's because powerful men made up that strong army. They were equipped for war and ready to defeat their adversaries. They engaged in the battle with the mentality they were going to defeat their opponent. They were ready to overpower their adversaries. They utilized their skills and their inner strength. Together strong minds and bodies created a powerful force. Their strategic movements helped them to maneuver the traps awaiting them.

Like soldiers, I've fought many battles but I've made it far enough to gain the victory. There were a lot of foggy days but when the smoke cleared even when I was mentally and physically wounded from the battle, I successfully carried out my mission.

I was preparing something big for quite a while and I figured it was time for the world to know the real deal about all the things that really went down. Now some people may have heard stories about me and decided to come to their own conclusions after watching how my character was depicted on the big screen but there's so much more details to share with you.

I decided to set the record straight after having people claiming to be me and after certain things being misconstrued, I thought it was time for people to know the real G'.The only way for people to know was for me to write a movie script on the account of my life and from there an autobiography.

I set everything into motion. I made a few phone calls to influential people which lead to lots of business meetings with the right individuals who could make it happen. Now I'm talking about people who deal with investments that have the power to make one phone call and it's done. I collaborated with music artists and record labels. I got in contact with directors, producers, writers and industry moguls. This is how everything fell into place.

I was in-between the negotiation process and contemplating who I was going to sign a contract with. There were a number of things to take into consideration, such as: percentages, experience, notoriety, accuracy, distribution and promotional strategies just to name a few.

Once I did all of the foot work, it was like the missing pieces to the puzzle came together. Investors were knocking at my door like crazy and everybody wanted in on this project. I didn't rush it and I refused to accept every offer that came my way.

In-between conference calls and business meetings, I narrowed it down to a few key players. All of which were knowledgeable of what it takes to complete a project and make it become a success.

The key players involved in this project were dedicated and committed from day one. That's when I knew it was my time. Let me explain how everything came to pass.

The first group of investors I was negotiating with was trying to get all rights to everything involving my project, plus an extra percentage! This means even if they didn't show up to set and had no involvement technically they would still get paid. Even if they didn't deserve an extra twenty percent, they would still get rights they were not respectfully entitled to. Can you believe that?

Mass media craves sex, violence, and drugs. Although my life entailed all of the above, I'm not condoning that type of lifestyle. In real life, when you know what it's like to live the fast life, you take so many risks. The fictional characters make it all look enjoyable even if you are being corrupted. The audience loves it and lives for the suspense. But in real life if you caught up in stuff you shouldn't be in you're in a dilemma trying to find a way out. Actors portray characters, and show you what it's like to look into the lifestyle that some people can only dream about. People pretended to be me, and emulate me, but now it's time for the world to see the real 'G.

I don't have to exaggerate anything. I know what it feels like to be infamous and have unlimited access to the material things of the world. But the truth stands. People need to see the light and accept things for what they are.

The completion of my project wouldn't be possible without the key players. Now let's talk about Mike. Mike is a genius. Along my journey, I met

Mike while he was shooting a film. Who would have known we'd be working on my projects years later!

From the first day when I met Mike, I saw that this educated man has ambition and drive. Mike specializes in the film industry. He has directed and produced film and TV and has contributed to many aspects of the entertainment industry. Mike started to work in partnership with me and he began to accompany me in my business endeavors. I started incorporating the art of negotiation with everyone I connected with. Things started flowing smoothly.

From that point on we were engaged in a lot of third party business calls. Negotiating with investors and arranging to meet with them. .

Through some close friends, I ended up meeting Tina. Tina is a very smart business woman who owns her own consultant /funding company with her business partner Tommy. She is highly respected worldwide and she is a producer, executive producer and director as well. Tina is instrumental in securing funding for large Independent Film projects in Hollywood. She also is a retired Vice President of a 100% children's charity. I was truly blessed when I met Tina. Later on, Tina becomes a very important part of my life.

Things started picking up so quickly once the right individuals were involved. So now there were more things to take into consideration, who would direct the movie? And who would portray the role of 'G.

I decided to go with a man that I consider to be a father figure to me. I chose Mr. D. My instincts told me he would be the most suitable individual to direct the movie and lead this film on redemption to fruition. Mr. D is a three-time Grammy winner. He is knowledgeable about industry standards, skillful and has the experience required for projecting and delivering my vision adequately. Mr. D directed 2 black Hollywood Films that are now classics. In addition, I believe in his ability to incorporate the mastermind principle into the movie and create a worldwide effect which will make this movie an instant success.

The search for talent and people will be from all across the world to be a part of the movie. Once we select the cast, more negotiations will come into play. I nominated Jamie Foxx to portray me. I believe he has the ability to deliver a strong and powerful performance.

I am in contact with Lynn the Publisher, The Lawyer in Atlanta, The Charlie's Angel guy in Canada, who is a director and owns a management company and the Hedge Fund man in Atlanta. All of which provided opportunities to advance this project and take the movie deal and the book deal to another level.

There are so many individuals who helped make everything come together. Its people like Monique, who owns a television and radio show who was a tremendous help. I commend her for her precision and intellect. She's such a detail oriented person. I appreciate what she brought to the table.

I am thankful for all of the other key players involved as well; people like Monica, Tye, The Jew, The German, The Italians, The Financial Consultants and the Lawyers that are all responsible for making things happen. From movie deals, to the book, marketing strategies, distribution, promotion, handling expenses, and everything else required for sponsorship. Because of the above mentioned people, I'm on my way to a movie deal. They believed in me and were willing to invest in my vision because they believed together we could generate a profit.

Chapter 32
Loyalty & Trust

Let's talk about trust and what it is to be loyal. You don't need a group of people to have loyalty. Loyalty can be between two people. It can be between a brother and a sister, a husband and a wife or two best friends. That's why it's important to understand what true loyalty is. In the matters of loyalty, one should never show dishonor. Some people say that they are loyal but they never hold up to their word when it's time to face the music.

True loyalty is when you can trust someone with your husband, wife, your money, all of your assets and even your life. In the matters of loyalty many are tested but not everyone passes the test. For example, look at all of these marriages that end up in divorce because of infidelity. Where is the loyalty? No it's not okay to be married and go creeping around looking for satisfaction in the comfort of another person's arms. The cheating game becomes the crying game. Then you got alimony. When kids are involved, child support, custody battles and war over who gets what property.

True loyalty would never be associated with distrust, deceit and all the things that transpire when there is lack of loyalty. How can you call yourself a brother and say that you're down for a person and then smile and their face and back stab them. That's "deception" in the mix. Some people can have a conversation with you and act like nothing's wrong. Then they turn around and act like a cut throat and spread crazy rumors about you. They do whatever they can in their will power to take you down and leave you left with nothing.

There are men behind bars today who are doing life in prison because the same person who said they were loyal snitched and broke the trust, the bond, the unity and the code after ratting their friend out. But loyalty doesn't work that way. If you say that you're loyal, even if you got to take the rap for your team...that is what loyalty is about. Some people got it all twisted. They claim they're loyal and they will be the first one going out like a sellout.

In an organization, there has to be loyalty. If you know specific details that nobody else knows about and your man gets caught up and all the heat and pressure is on you...that don't mean it's time to fold up under pressure and rat him out. Why would you rat him out if that's your right hand man? You know some people just don't know what loyalty is. They have no idea what the true meaning of trust and loyalty represents. They talk a good one but don't walk the walk. The truth is true loyalty means no matter what the consequences are, you would never betray that person or do anything to jeopardize the status of your relationship with that person.

I once heard a story about this Madame who gave millions of dollars to this guy. When he started working for her he had nothing, but he blew up and became big time after she put him on. But, in the end, he betrayed her. As a result of his disloyalty, she sent people to come looking for him. He escaped after almost losing his life behind his betrayal. She made him who he had become, but yet he failed the test of loyalty and trust.

Even the government has to appoint trusted individuals. The president has to have trust in his cabinet member and share an oath of loyalty and they have the responsibility of being dependable at all times. No matter what, every organization is based on loyalty and trust. In the mafia there must be guaranteed loyalty. If you're in the military fighting a war, you have to trust in the military guys in your atmosphere to watch your back and guard your life. Someone can be in attack mode and ready to strike when you're not looking and that is where loyalty and trust comes into play. Do you trust a person enough with your life? Will they be your shield and protection if you're assigned to fight on the battlefield?

You see most people just talk but your actions will show your true character. You can speak like you are concerned and devoted to a person but when situations come about the truth will find out your true intentions. When you meet someone in life, every person always haves something on their agenda for you, but the question is what? You need to ask yourself this question and seriously analyze it. Out of all the people in your circle, how many people can you depend on? Who do you think will be there for you if you ever were in need? You know it's always the people you least expect who proves their loyalty.

Loyalty and trust is very important. But it's a shame when a person can't trust you, because in initializing any type of relationship, whether it's business, platonic, romantic, or relative related...you have to establish some form of trust from day one. All you have to go by is the person's word. So if they break that bond of trust they clarify their disloyalty.

There are people today who are still hurting inside because of someone who broke their trust and were not loyal. That's messed up! You have men who got cheated on and women whose men went with their best friends, husbands who found their wives in bed with another man and wives who caught their husband's cheating and having multiple affairs with different women. What this does is make people live with doubt and they live in fear. Then become afraid that everyone will lie to them and that everyone will hurt them so they end up going into defense mode and want to hurt people who don't have anything to do with what happened to them. It's time for people to get a reality check. You can't go on for the rest of your life blaming the innocent for what another person did to you. You're mad because of all of the hurt and can't believe that they betrayed you, but you have to get over it. You have to let go of the past. It's over and done with. Just let go and move on. Okay, so you found out the person wasn't who they said they were. But you know what? I believe they did you a favor.

It's a good thing to find out the true character of the person that you're dealing with. So for all of you people out there who have been hurt and betrayed; you have to realize how blessed you are that person is out of your life and you no longer have to deal with the stress and aggravation anymore. Now there is a burden and weight lifted off your shoulders. So focus on you. There are some people who are just not cut out for loyalty because they work in treachery. It's going to be okay as long as you motivate yourself and then learn the lesson behind what occurred. Sometimes things are only meant to prepare you for the better things on the road ahead. In order to get those things, those negative people have to be removed from your life because they were only blocking you and hindering you.

Have you ever been loyal? Are you trustworthy and dedicated to those around you? I know what it means to keep the loyalty flowing. It's a life time partnership and obligation and you have to treat it like a marriage. It's like taking a vow and that vow is not meant to be broken until separation by death. Some people make vows and swear under oath but loyalty is the final determination of where you will stand and show to what degree you can put your trust in that person. It's not about what you say. It's all about what you do. Remember, it's your actions that people see. So no matter how sincere a person may seem and if the evidence shows proof that they are not keeping it real, then you already know what time it is. At that point, there is nothing else to question. Once you have your answer, the next move you should be making is" breaking free."

If you see you got people in your circle that are no good and not capable of being loyal, then your next move and your best move is to prepare for your exit strategy. You don't have to make a blatant announcement that you're "through" with the person and that That you know they betrayed you and that their no good. Sometimes silence is the best remedy. If you're low key, then there's no telling what you're doing in life. They cannot hurt you anymore. But remember if a person can't be trusted, then end of story...say good-bye...sayonara as the Japanese would say.

You know in order to be where I am today; I had to endure the test of loyalty and trust. I had to see if the people I was affiliated with fit the criteria of being loyal and trustworthy. Including the individuals I'm associated with had to know that I was capable of keeping my end of the bargain. Along the way, I also had to do the process of elimination, by distancing myself from the type of influences that were not showing any indication of loyalty. Although they portrayed themselves to be those types of people that were reliable. When I got away from that element of letting people like that drain my energy, I became focused and resilient. This enabled me to concentrate on areas of my life which entitled me to discover the level and placed me in the position of landing a movie deal.

Chapter 33

The Movie

After entering into a joint business venture, I decided it was time to set the record straight once and for all. A lot of different people painted different pictures of me according to hearsay and their own notions. They don't know the real G Money. Some people depicted me as a "monster" because of all of this talk about me. Believe it or not, there are guys claiming to be me. They used my name because they were idolizing the character portrayed. But I don't condone some of the things I've done. I'm not glorifying things that can cause suffering and pain.

The man that I am today has made a transition from my old way of thinking. If anything, I want to see the people in my community expand and have abundance. I don't want to put stumbling blocks before my brothers and sisters. So I decided to share my life story and tell some of the most intimate details that most people don't know about me. To educate the youth and let them see by the mistakes I made. Hopefully, they won't take the same route it took.

The route I took is not for everyone. Some people are in the grave today because of living the street life. And some people think that kind of lifestyle is fascinating but that's no way to live man.

When you walk in the streets, anybody could be watching you The Feds, DT's and informers. Including all of the snitches wanting to get in on what you worked so hard for. It's not easy. It's a lot of cut throats out there and sly talkers that will try to put you out of commission altogether.

Every time I stepped on the scene, I was prepared for anything because at any given moment something could go down and things could get ballistic.

The drug world can be very malicious and heartless. It's strictly cold blooded and brutal to the core. It's not cut out for everyone. When you enter that world you're taking a tremendous risk.

Society and the media depict their picture of what that life is like, but you don't really know unless you've been in that world. It's nothing like your imagination or assumptions. It's the real deal. If you have to take drastic measures to prove your point, you got to do it. If you get sent to take care of business, you better not come up short. You better not get caught by the cops. If you got locked up, you're on your own!

You will see who got your back and who's in your corner when you're doing time. It will be the people you least expect who hold you down and give you commissary. But while you locked up, that's time wasted that you don't get back. Plus you got to deal with goons on the inside. Inmates plotting to catch another victim and cats trying to test your weaknesses. If you get intimidated and can't deter yourself or role with somebody that got your back, you're screwed. Just like a fish in a shark tank. You'll get eaten alive.

When I left that lifestyle, I took a look at today's generation and most of these cats out here are lost. They need structure. There walking around thinking that they impress somebody but they just look foolish and they don't even know it.

By the grace of God, I've been redeemed and I realized the importance of sharing my life story with the generation of today. If you have the opportunity to get your education and do things the legitimate way don't be persuaded by the crowd. You can have all the finer things in life without going down the wrong path to obtain it. You just have to work hard for it and believe in yourself.

It's been a long run from entering the game to getting out of the game. It has come to a point in life where you look back and come to the conclusion that you could have done things differently but just chose not to. Back then everything was just for the moment. The difference now is that I see far beyond the momentary thrills and pleasures offered by the world. I operate by purpose and intent now and I think about the repercussions that follow my actions. I won't indulge in anything that I know is not productive and I won't introduce anything to my body that's toxic and can jeopardize my well-being.

When I layed low, I was M.I.A. for a while and folks were making all types of speculations about me. They thought they knew all the details, but if you want answers you got to go to the main source.

All along, no one had a clue what was really going on because I was low key. No one knew that I was busy making the preparations to build my empire. I was gearing up to enter into new business ventures and meeting with

208

lawyers, executives and investors. I had editors, photographers, and producers contacting me, everyone was waiting for me to tell my story.

It's time to show the brothers and sisters of today; you can escape from the limitations and barricades of the streets, the system and the ongoing conspiracy of the worldly operation.

If you pay close attention and learn from experience by what I share with you and make some adjustments in your life to areas that need change; you will see that you have other options as well. If you change your way of thinking and change your circle just like I did, you can become a millionaire.

You can have your own business and be your own boss. If you are confident and believe in yourself and want to pursue your dreams people will invest in you. You will attract wealth and will make business connections with billionaires and millionaires just like me.

It all depends on your choices and your mind set. I already told myself that I was aiming for millionaire status and I did not stop until I made it happen.

You see I already envisioned myself with the wealth in advance. I already claimed that abundant living was mines and that I would obtain it. I believed it was only a matter of time and I never was a quitter and that's how I will become a multi-millionaire.

I didn't skip a beat. I hit every note in exercising my authority of which I was given. That puts the "S" on my chest. God put the "Super" on my natural body. This was my

Chapter 34

How I Became a Success

From a young age, I was surrounded by wealth. I can recall watching high rollers pull up in fancy cars and walking proudly with their women, wearing expensive fur coats. I saw men that were dressed to the 9's and their diamonds and jewels were so flashy you could spot it from a mile away. I thought to myself, "One day I'll be big time just like that".

Momma exposed me to all of the finer things in life. So I already had the concept to set high standards for myself. She showed me what it was like to have strictly the best, so I kept in mind never to settle for less.

I was introduced to the lavish lifestyle at an early stage in my life. My friends and I were accustomed to getting chauffeured around on the regular. While our limousine drivers took us to our destination, we always got V.I.P. treatment wherever we went. We attracted wealth, beautiful women and moved like a conglomerate while we made a reputation for ourselves. Whenever we stepped on the scene you could tell we were getting money automatically because our attire said it all. Everything we wore was exclusive.

It felt good to have thousands of dollars in my pocket. Whatever I wanted I got it and I didn't have to worry about looking at the price tag, I could afford it and I was in the position to spend as much as I pleased. If I wanted to splurge that wasn't an issue for me there was more money piling up in my stash, which was always accessible.

Once you experience what it feels like to be wealthy and be a part of the elite society, there are no limits on the things that you can obtain. When you have connections and well-off friends it makes a huge difference.

The lavish lifestyle comes with a lot of perks. You have unlimited access to everything that a man could ever desire. What makes a huge difference is when you have the right connections and friends who can pull a couple of strings and make sure that you're straight concerning whatever you need. You become exposed to so many things when you have friends that are members of the elite society. It's an eye opener when you travel and see people who are living comfortably. They are not struggling and don't have to work from check to check to make ends meet.

Once you experience what it feels like to be wealthy, there are certain standards that you set for yourself because you're used to having whatever you crave for when you want it. But when you lose all that you had and you're without, you get a burning desire to get back on that level. You will do what it takes to reach that level of success again.

After I fell, I experienced the limitations of the obstacles that prevent you from moving ahead. I lost a lot of things, so I ended up right back at square one. But I knew I wouldn't stay down for long. Every day I devised a plan and the end result would lead me to accomplishing my goal of becoming a millionaire and once again being back on top.

I reached out to all of my connections, all of which are financially established. I started making propositions and proposals. I knew somebody that I was affiliated with would be interested in what I had to bring to the table. It was only a matter of time.

Once I took the initiative and made an effort and wasn't sitting around waiting for someone to do everything for me, the calls started coming in like clockwork. I was now in the position to accept or decline an offer, because God made it possible for me. Doorways to opportunities keep opening up. At one point, there were so many business deals lined up that I got overwhelmed. I remained focused.

The mastermind took charge and then I incorporated all of my mastermind techniques to my strategy. Then I thought about all of the powerful and successful men in the world. They all had certain structure. They were people in high positions that they were connected to who were the main reason they reached a level of empowerment. They didn't do it all alone. It starts with your idea, and then you need someone in your circle to assist you in manifesting your vision. So I put together the round table, each individual specializes in a specific area in the industry. They were all dedicated team players.

As I watched things unfold, I was looking at Million dollar contracts and sealing deals with entities that were willing to invest in my projects and my visions. Where are all of my dreamers? I never stopped pushing my dreams forward. You have to keep your dreams alive until you birth them. Once I kept my dreams alive and kept pushing to manifest them my dreams became a reality.

Then the money started flowing from every direction. Talk shows, radio shows and magazine companies were all interested in interviewing me to hear about my story. They are still banging my door down!

Things started moving rapidly. What would have happened if I would have given up? Do you know where I could have been if I stopped believing? That was not an option. I am the man with a strong will and a burning desire to succeed.

I know what it feels like when determination is your driver, ambition is your keys and perseverance is your ignition. I refused to be mentally weakened or lost in mental slavery and fall victim to the limitations of society. I am now free of lack. I have a multitude of increase and more than I've ever had in my life and this is only the beginning.

It doesn't stop here. I have more to accomplish and more information to share. But the brothers and sisters of today must be willing to learn... Take it from an O'G. I know what it's like to have money, power and respect. But if you don't get your mind right, stay on point and do things right away, you'll end up lost and find yourself in a vicious cycle where the strong will excel and the weak will diminish. If people are not cautious, they while be trapped in a world where predators are savages to their prey and hunters will be waiting for their target.

So you must always keep your guards up, don't ever get caught sleeping. Stay on point at all times. That's why I always kept my eyes open. You have to be able to read people and see through them. You have to know peoples intentions before they even make their moves so you will be prepared and already placed in a position where you have the upper hand. That way you will call the shots and the ball will be in your court. You have to keep close watch like you're watching your opponent before they strike. Remember what I said. Act like the feds are watching you.

Somebody is always watching...There will be a "Red Carpet Event" the night of my book release and The Cash Money Brothers and Sisters will come together like never before.

We move like a firm and the haters can't take it. There will be lights flashing and cameras all over. Reporters, interviewers, photographers, spectators and members of the elite society will be on the scene looking exuberant, elegant and stunning as they magnetize everyone in sight.

I already can feel the intensity of the haters and their envious glare, but this is only the beginning of a Powerhouse Movement on the rise.

Chapter 35

The Red Carpet
Book Release Event

It's almost time! All of the blood, sweat, and tears has paid off. I paid my dues and ran the good race. I fought many battles. There were times when I lost and days when I failed but I kept on fighting until I came out with the victory.

Through perseverance, determination and a strong desire to succeed I came out a winner! Now, after all the hard work, it has come time for recognition and to show my appreciation. Finally, I've reached the end result of my vision. I never gave up and kept pushing my dreams until they manifested.

As I took a look at all of the individuals around me, I thought of how grateful I was for all of the dedication and team effort it took to make everything come together... and so it came to pass.

Soon, it will be the night that everyone was waiting for. The spectacular "Red Carpet" event. This night will be like no other! It will be the greatest moment of my life. It will be the night of my book release! There will be Sparkling lights and cameras flashing everywhere! The paparazzi will be on the move trying to get the best picture of Hollywood's most elite celebrities and moguls form the entertainment industry!

Limousines, Lamborghinis and all type of luxury cars will be pulling up out front. I can see it now! It will be a most mesmerizing moment! It will be so wonderful, I will finally be speechless!

Spectators will glance from afar to see who is being interviewed by members of the press. Everyone will be curious to know all of the nitty-gritty about the return of G Money, the book: Rebirth for Redemption, the movie deal and all of the details about New York's Own, as I now introduce the New Motown; the new music singing sensations and the next generation of the music era!

This is my greatest moment as the spotlight will shine in my direction! Now I now think to myself "This is the manifestation of a mastermind." As I transition into an overnight success story, I just know that the book sales will go through the roof!

The recipe for success comes according to your belief. I can't stress that enough. I see so many fail because they lack faith and don't believe in their self. If you have a vision you can make it into a reality and become part of that 1% that I mentioned before.

As I look at all of the powerful individuals in my atmosphere today, I think about the art of persistence. I am surrounded by the rich and elite, but that's only because I never gave up and I never burned my bridges. You got to be careful how you treat folks. People will remember and your reputation is everything, especially in the Entertainment industry. I never burned my bridges. I never forgot about the people who helped me to get to where I am today and I never backstabbed anyone to get to this point.

I know that in order to be blessed, I had to bless somebody else first. It's a chain reaction. What you put out there is what you get back in return. And most important, I put away all of the things of the old... like bad habits, bad influences and things that I needed to remove from my way of living. I walk in newness; it's a new day and it's time for new beginnings!

There are so many people who stood in my corner during some of the most difficult times but they helped me to get through it. And you know what? Come to think of it, it's funny how people thought I vanished and moved to another country when I was M.I.A. There was all kind of rumors circulating out there! You can't believe all that hype about events that took place during the New Jack era. Till this very day, people still wonder about certain things I did and said. People still believe that I probably fell off! I didn't fall off track. I'm still standing and living better than ever!!

I did step off the scene for a minute, but I never left. I was always in the mix, moving like the James Bond of Harlem, 007 status! I was on a mission with a continuous will to survive, defeat and complete what I came to do.

When you see me now, take a close look at me! I stand, born again, "Resurrected & Redeemed" shifting to other stages. I am on the next level now. I have made it to a higher plateau because I was determined to get there one way or the other. And see, the haters couldn't stop me!

I learned how to break through the barriers of life that are meant to leave you in bondage, chained and enslaved. Why limit yourself? There are so

214

many things in this world for you to explore, but if you stay trapped in a mind frame where you allow limitations to overpower your circumstances, than you will only experience what you are making your expectations.

Take it from me and stop limiting yourself. Learn from my mistakes and my life story. I still made it regardless of all of the obstacles and complicated circumstances that I faced in life. I refused to be a quitter and so can you because a winner will not quit.

I will not lose and I will not fail this time around. I use to be broken down and torn apart inside, the troubles of the world were making my soul weary but I couldn't let go...I knew that my future was bright, although the light around me was diming. Can you imagine what would have happened if I would have given up? I wasn't going out like that under any circumstance. I knew I was going to come up and be back on top. I knew better things were headed in my direction. It can happen for you too, but let me tell you one thing; you better keep dreaming and believing that you'll recover from your past woes. When you stop believing and you give up hope, that's when you become a failure. So don't think you can't....think "I CAN".

I have the greatest gift a man could ever have in this life. The love of God is with me and you too...even if you don't believe. I'm going to continue to move in greatness and it doesn't stop here. There's more to come as the chronicles continue...

I remain the ORIGINAL "Gerald G. Money".......

SEE YOU AT THE RED CARPET BOOK RELEASE PARTY!!